ON
GANDHI'S
PATH

Stephanie Mills has described Bob Swan's life with eloquence, elegance and profoundness and as a result the book is deeply engaging and enchanting. *On Gandhi's Path* is a lucid narrative of the life of Bob Swann who was a living example of simplicity, humility and radicalism. This is a book which describes how a man offered himself to serve the people and the planet selflessly. This book is a good guide to all activists who are working to transform the world.

— Satish Kumar, editor, *Resurgence Magazine* and
Visiting Fellow at Schumacher College

Bob Swann was the unsung American Gandhi. He was a pioneer in intentional communities, local currencies, populist architecture, cooperatives, radical decentralization, land trusts, draft resistance, and antiwar activism. Stephanie Mills's biography exquisitely fills the historical void, showing how much a humble but determined individual could transform American life and reminding us of many of our ideals are still possible.

— Michael Shuman, author, *The Small-Mart Revolution*

One of the great unrecognized heroes of the 20th century decentralist movement, Bob Swann here gets the careful, serious, and may I say loving, treatment he deserves.

— Kirkpatrick Sale, co-founder, E.F. Schumacher Society,
and author, *Human Scale*

On Gandhi's Path is the definitive, long-anticipated biography of Robert Swann, peace activist, economic reformer, writer, critic, scholar, social investor, builder, carpenter, family-man, visionary and my friend. We are fortunate that another visionary pioneer, Stephanie Mills tells this fascinating story.

— Hazel Henderson, author, *Ethical Markets*

Stephanie Mills has reached into a forgotten part of history – the part where they put the plain spoken, the honest and simple, the peaceful tillers of the earth – and retrieved a relevant saint for our time. To the seven billion of us, hard up against converging consequences of horrendously bad choices made at a global scale, Bob Swann speaks, through his articulate and poetic biographer, of the way out. That path is lit, not with dangling ornaments of consumerism, militant fireworks, or grand political theater, but by Swann's lantern, held aloft by dint of his own life, revealing appropriately sensitive local economy and elegantly responsive local choice.

— Albert Bates, permaculture instructor and author,
The Post-Petroleum Survival Guide and Cookbook and
Atmosphere or Agriculture: Carbon Farming and Climate Change

ON GANDHI'S PATH

*Bob Swann's Work for Peace
and Community Economics*

Stephanie Mills

NEW SOCIETY PUBLISHERS

Cataloging in Publication Data:
A catalog record for this publication is available from
the National Library of Canada.

Cover design by Diane McIntosh.
Cover photos © Michael Silverwise msilverwise@hotmail.com.

First printing March 2010.

Paperback ISBN: 978-0-86571-615-5

Inquiries regarding requests to reprint all or part of
On Gandhi's Path should be addressed to
New Society Publishers at the address below.

To order directly from the publishers,
please call toll-free (North America) 1-800-567-6772,
or order online at www.newsociety.com

Any other inquiries can be directed by mail to:
New Society Publishers
P. O. Box 189, Gabriola Island, BC V0R 1X0, Canada
(250) 247-9737

New Society Publishers' mission is to publish books that contribute in
fundamental ways to building an ecologically sustainable and just society,
and to do so with the least possible impact on the environment, in a manner
that models this vision. New Society also works to reduce its carbon
footprint, and purchases carbon offsets based on an annual audit to ensure
a carbon neutral footprint. For further information, or to browse our full list
of books and purchase securely, visit our website at: www.newsociety.com

NEW SOCIETY PUBLISHERS
www.newsociety.com

Contents

Preface and Acknowledgments

When, in 1999, Susan Witt, the executive director of the E.F. Schumacher Society and Bob Swann's life partner, invited me to work with Bob on his biography I was honored and instantly agreed. I knew and admired both Bob and Susan and was grateful for their endeavors in the world. Learning more about Bob's works and days and helping to convey his story to readers was a rewarding prospect.

Before I was able to begin our collaboration Bob completed his book *Peace, Civil Rights, and the Search for Community*. It was posted on the Schumacher Society's website and is well worth reading.[1] In 2001 with support from a patron of the Schumacher Society, I was able to spend a month interviewing Bob, surveying the Society's archives and outlining a book. In 2003 Bob died, leaving us to celebrate his life and mourn its ending. Although this book had yet to find its publisher, Susan's encouragement of the project was unwavering. Absent a publisher, my plan was to write four long essays about Bob's life work that the Schumacher Society could publish, perhaps as part of its pamphlet series. Together the essays might someday constitute a book. One of the essays, "Bob Swann's 'Positively Dazzling Realism,'"[2] was delivered at the Schumacher Society's 24th annual lectures and has been published as a pamphlet. Another, "Young Vigor Searching for Light,"[3] was posted on the Society's website.

In 2004 this rookie biographer had the incalculable good fortune to begin a correspondence with Paul Salstrom, an historian who had known and worked with Bob during the 1960s and 1970s.

Salstrom generously copied sheaves of relevant material from his own archives, obtained scholarly articles, commented on drafts of the manuscript and offered his own recollections and insights. He has been a wonderfully responsive and supportive pen pal throughout the project.

Also in 2004, The Mesa Refuge in Point Reyes, California provided me with a month's residency. A seaside conversation there with the founder Peter Barnes, an entrepreneur and writer on matters economic, helped steer my work. The Mesa Refuge not only gave me a beautiful perch in the company of fellow writers but a base whence I could venture out to interview Bob's former wife Marjorie Swann Edwin and their four children Dhyana, Judy, Carol and Scott all of whom lived in northern California. On several occasions over the course of this work Bob's brother Jim Swann took the time to speak with me. Jim kindly provided copies of letters Bob wrote him from prison as well as some photographs. Richard King, the late Dhyana Swann's husband, also helped provide photographs.

In 2005, Christopher Plant at New Society offered to publish the book before you. As a stalwart of the bioregionalist movement, Plant was aware of Bob Swann's work in community economics and its relevance to the ecosocial movement lately being called relocalization. New Society's recognition of the importance of a book on Bob Swann's life and work crystallized the project — and gave it an actual deadline.

By 2008, it was necessary to find further funding to complete the work on the book. Harriet Barlow, director of the Blue Mountain Center, put out an appeal on behalf of the Swann Book Project. A score of friends generously responded. Thanks to Katie Alvord and Kraig Klungness, Ernest Callenbach and Christine Leefeldt, Fritjof Capra, Jim Crowfoot, John Diamante, Suzi Gablik, David Haenke, John Knott, Barry Lopez and Debra Gwartney, the Leslie Jones Foundation, Jerry Mander, Bill McKibben and Sue Halpern, Tad Montgomery, Coco and Roger Newton, Christina Rawley and

Ron Zweig, Paul Salstrom, Tom and Darylene Shea and the Tides Foundation for the gifts that kept the lights on and the author fed.

That summer Jonathan Cobb, a consummate bookman, bestowed another vital gift in volunteering to read and comment on the manuscript. Ingrid Witvoet, managing editor at New Society shepherded the book and offered sage pep talks to the author. Betsy Nuse, the copy editor, nicely groomed the prose. Boundless gratitude to all the members of the village that it took to raise this book!

In the years since Bob Swann's death, the Schumacher Society which he and Susan founded has continued to develop its usefulness to a worldwide community of individuals and organizations seeking practical, moral alternatives to heedless gargantuan economics as usual. The Society's most celebrated recent accomplishment was its successful launch of *BerkShares*, a local currency. To date millions of dollars in local exchange has been conducted in BerkShares. BerkShares rapidly became an inspiring model for scores of other local currencies, drawing thousands of inquiries to the Schumacher Society website.

Out of the limelight and quite as important is the ongoing intellectual community organizing that Witt and her colleagues at the Schumacher Society do through their research, education and consultation. To learn more about Schumacher Society activities and resources, visit their website smallisbeautiful.org or write to the E. F. Schumacher Society, 140 Jug End Road, Great Barrington, Massachusetts, 01230 USA.

Robert Swann: An Appreciation

From my several encounters with Bob Swann, beginning about 1980, I have a good many memories of him that are dear to me. What I know from all of them is that he was never a man who in any way falsified or misrepresented himself in order to "make an impression." Or, to put it a different way, your "impression" of him after you had known him for a few hours would stand the test of knowing him for twenty years.

The memory of him that I like most comes from a meeting we both attended in Dallas. Bob's assignment was a panel discussion, which took place in a small theater in the center of town. The other members of the panel were a couple of Dallas businessmen and the head of one of the New York stock exchanges — pretty high-powered company, it seemed to me.

I was anxious for Bob, because in such circumstances I would have been anxious for myself. But Bob sat on the stage with the outward quiet that can come only from inward quiet. He listened courteously to the other people throughout. He didn't object, correct, or otherwise interrupt. When his turn came to speak, he said his say quietly, confidently, kindly, modestly, with candor and clarity, and without any open acknowledgement that what he was saying was opposed to anything that the others had said. Right in front of the financial Bigtime and its inflated optimism, he simply stood his argument on its legs, backed away, and let it stand.

He was speaking, of course, of the importance of local economy, local credit, local currency. And I remember the gratitude — the great respect and love — I felt for what he was saying, and for what he was.

Introduction

A DIVERSE GROUP OF GREAT if marginalized thinkers — some compassionate, some outraged, some spiritually motivated and some who were simply wise observers — have addressed the interlinked problems of community scale and self-determination; of land ownership and the creation of money; of locating social justice and a common prosperity. They have regarded nationalism as a scourge, seen that excessive size in countries or institutions or polities bespeaks aggression. Out of their conviction that people can and will take care of themselves and their neighbors when cultural and economic forms encourage such face-to-face responsibility, a philosophy has emerged — call it decentralism, local self-reliance or mutual aid.

This book concerns one of those decentralists, Bob Swann. A pioneer of community economics, Bob Swann (1918–2003) was also a peace activist. Swann was not a revolutionary. Nor was he particularly — or merely — political. He was a true radical. Swann's vision emerged in the 20th century when the human enterprise had created pockets of cozy prosperity and allowed outbreaks of liberation but also had generated nightmares of total war.

Swann's life work, critically informed by the American experience of the 1930s and 1940s and by Gandhi's philosophy and methods, always sought the root of any problem. The locality —

town, city, neighborhood and region — was, as Swann and all decentralists understood, the nexus of the common weal. Accordingly, Swann focused on empowering individuals and communities through the creation of small-scale, self-help institutions. Swann forged tools to build productive, resilient local and regional economies.

From the tutelage in philosophy and literature he received as an adolescent from a Lutheran pastor in Cleveland Heights, Ohio, to the classes he audited at Ohio State University, to the reading he did while he was in prison for draft resistance right on up to the articles on novel energy sources on his desk in 2001, Bob's intellectual activity was constant. If this book is more about the ideas than the man, it's because Bob lived his ideas. Although he didn't lack insight or empathy, he was not interested overmuch in the depths of anyone's psychology or personality, not even his own.

Without simply recapitulating it, *On Gandhi's Path* follows, amplifies and adds detail to the story Bob tells in his own autobiography, *Peace, Civil Rights, and the Search for Community*. To do this, I chose to rely primarily on written and published sources. Although the annals of Bob's times engrossed me and the historical impulse took hold, I have written as a journalist rather than as an historian or economist. An exhaustive biography would have been beyond both my knowledge and the assignment. Because I too am a species of decentralist, my appreciation of Swann's work will be obvious.

A visionary for his time and ours, Bob Swann was articulate, creative, prolific and, for decades of his life, right in the thick of historic social movements. To try, with any number of words, to do justice to such a person's life is humbling. Perhaps the difficulty of selecting the most salient aspects of such an engaged life is just the biographical version of the agony of art: the work will always fall short of full portraiture.

On Gandhi's Path begins with a consideration of community economics, for that is the field where Bob Swann did his most useful work. Just past the midpoint in his life Swann discovered his aptitude and passion for economic reform. His decentralism was cardinal. Without cant or exhortation, Swann improved the morality, by recalibrating the optimum scale, of various economic endeavors. Now as global industrial civilization flails in the throes of an ecological and economic crisis, Swann's working innovations are at the ready to help neighborhoods, local entrepreneurs and willing communities with an ethic of mutual aid to rebuild at appropriate scales.

Bob Swann was born comfortably middle class in 1918. The first chapter of this book outlines his early years. Precociously independent, he clashed with his father early on. Regardless, he enjoyed his childhood in a convivial neighborhood next to a woodland that afforded a freedom just right for kids. The Swann family was affected by the Great Depression, but nobody starved. Straitened circumstances meant that Bob wound up living like a bohemian while he audited classes at Ohio State University. It was there, as America's entry into World War II drew nigh, that he decided to resist the draft. His absolutism led to a stint in prison and to decades of peace activism thereafter.

War resistance in the US called for uncommon courage and adamant principle. Its history is too little known. Chapter 3 begins with a glimpse at that history, for radical pacifism shaped Swann's life. Gandhi galvanized the thinking of the American peace activists of Bob's younger days. Honoring Gandhi's *two-legged strategy*, American radical pacifism concerned itself as much with the creation of social alternatives — racial integration among them — as it did with the refusal to participate in war. Incarcerated conscientious objectors (COs), Swann's cohorts, teemed with ideas for a positive future.

Like war resistance, decentralism has a substantial, if little known, history in America. While Bob Swann was in prison for noncompliance with the draft, Arthur Morgan, a prominent decentralist author and educator, offered the conscientious objectors a correspondence course on the small community. Bob became a star pupil. To introduce today's readers to some of the earlier literature of decentralism, not least Morgan's work, an account of that course makes up much of the fourth chapter of this book.

After getting out of prison Bob Swann married Marjorie Shaffer, a fellow pacifist. The Swanns proceeded to live an unorthodox, activist version of the postwar years. Bob began his career as a designer and builder of residences. It was a time when the cooperative movement was vibrant, involving a whole range of people who were looking for economic alternatives to capitalism and collectivism. Bob and Marj gravitated to a cooperative center in Southwest Michigan, making one of their innumerable households nearby. As the suburban 1950s unfolded, the young family grew to four children. Bob's work on vanguard interracial housing led them to Philadelphia. There, wife and motherhood notwithstanding, Marj Swann gained renown for nonviolent resistance. The most celebrated of these actions resulted in her imprisonment. Chapter 5 concerns, in part, the Swanns' eventful home life within the peace movement.

The 1960s found the Swanns going deeper into the movement, leaving behind their ranch style [anti]nuclear family home near Philadelphia to lead a peace commune near Voluntown, Connecticut. This intentional community was, depending on your standpoint, noble or notorious. Voluntown was the place where Bob Swann began to implement his economic innovations and is the setting of the book's sixth chapter. War protest and civil rights activism were entwined there and called forth brave witness year after year. Time spent on interracial building projects in the Jim Crow South spurred Bob's thinking on land tenure and community development. The community land trust movement, a voluntary approach to lasting land reform and Bob's signal achievement, was conceived at Voluntown in the late 1960s. Swann's design included community participation in chartering the use of the land, which is held as a trust by a nonprofit corporation.

Bob Swann's decentralism, land trust and civil rights work led to his collegial relationship with Ralph Borsodi, an economic consultant, educator and by the late 1960s, a decentralist elder. Swann and Borsodi collaborated on ingenious rural development programs that were linked to bold ideas in monetary reform. Chapter 7 glosses this wide-ranging work. An experimental issue of *Constants*, a commodities-indexed, non-inflating currency, found ready acceptance in Borsodi's Exeter, New Hampshire hometown.

Swann's experience with the Constant equipped him to become a mentor to the local currency revival of the 1980s. The flurry of interest in new money was catalyzed in part by the multipurpose E. F. Schumacher Society which Swann co-founded with Susan Witt, who was a teacher and community organizer. Located on a community land trust in the Southern Berkshires region of Massachusetts, the Schumacher Society was Swann's home and workplace until the last months of his life. The final chapter of the book, then, concerns the Schumacher Society. Through the Society, Swann and Witt spurred self-help economics in the Berkshires and beyond. Together for more than 20 years Swann and Witt originated practical local programs and propagated decentralist thinking to advance an "economics as if people mattered." When Bob Swann died in 2003, his last public utterances weren't elegiac or valedictory but encouragement to others to keep refining and practicing specific actions in local economic development. Today Susan Witt, his equal in insight and zeal for the transformation of economics, carries forward the E. F. Schumacher Society's increasingly relevant work.

CHAPTER 1

A Visionary for Our Time

Hope remains only in the most difficult task of all:
to reconsider everything from the ground up,
so as to shape a living society inside a dying society.

Albert Camus, "Neither Victims nor Executioners"[1]

URING THE WRITING OF THIS BOOK, which began in 2001, events moved very fast, accelerating in 2008 and 2009 when the manuscript was finished. The collapse of the global economy, which Bob Swann and his mentor Ralph Borsodi had anticipated, seemed imminent. There's no telling what will have happened in the interval between completion of the book and its publication. Given the ecological crises that loom along with a worldwide recession, a return to our accustomed way of life seems unlikely. Which may not be all bad news. The global economy has not served the planet or the majority of its people terribly well. Now, with that economy's possible demise we are, as the cartoon sage Pogo Possum put it, "confronted by insurmountable opportunities."

Bob Swann died a little too soon to help confront these opportunities. His genius for community economics would come in handy right now, not to mention his experience in civil disobedience, for it still takes a mighty clamor for certain views to get a hearing. But Swann slipped the mortal coil a few years before the greed-spawned debacle of finance capital, fiat money, credit-fueled consumerism and real estate speculation pushed industrial civilization to the brink.

Having foreseen the possibility of such a calamity, Swann spent the latter part of his life creating appropriately scaled, participatory forms of land reform, credit and money — local antidotes to centripetal economics. The institutions Bob Swann crafted, or helped to develop — like community land trusts, socially responsible investing, micro-lending and local currency — already have lives of their own in communities throughout North America and will doubtless find more opportunity as the center fails to hold.

Bob Swann and I last spoke in the early days of the George W. Bush administration, before the US had invaded Iraq, at a time when the nation's economy was, if not actually in decent shape, still plausible. I wish I could interview him today. I would love to hear Bob's appraisal of Wall Street's phantasmagoria and more of his recollections from his youth in the Great Depression. Beyond that, I would like to be around his good temperament. The years had taught him a lot. He wasn't given to panic or enmity. Prophets stand outside of history, advocating right conduct regardless of circumstances. Bob Swann had that sort of steadfastness.

"The human race may not survive," Bob said one day when we were discussing the prospects. "There's a good probability. So what are you going to do — become a fascist?"[2]

Only a few days after I had mostly wrapped up my interviews with Bob at his apartment in an assisted living facility in Lenox, Massachusetts and gone to Cape Cod for a visit with friends, the terrorist attacks on New York City and Washington DC occurred. September 11, 2001 and the subsequent pileup of ecological and political crises since then have demonstrated the problematical nature of hypercomplex centralized systems and far-flung, energy intensive trade.

Although those conversations with Bob were less than a decade ago, it feels like an era gone by. The economic ideology of growth for the sake of growth has nearly razed the planet. The time is overripe for a radical reappraisal of our economic practices and purposes. Husbanding the land and retaining locally created wealth to foster regional economies centered on the sustainable production of basic necessities may prove to be more viable paths than further industrialization, urbanization and globalization.

If new kinds of societies are to rise within the crumbling shell of the old, we will have to build them, part by part. Swann was a builder by trade and by nature. He enjoyed design, construction and good work. He brought that sensibility to his projects in community economics, devising elements that would work — provided that community members wanted to join the effort and invest some time and resources of their own.

All too often, leaders are people who write checks that other peoples' bodies will have to cash. The more exalted the leader, the more bodies bear the consequences of the leaders' directives, of their action or inaction. The more distant the authority is from the locale, the less sensitive and intelligent its directives are apt to be. It seems that worthy leadership is not so much the power to send others forward as to go forward oneself in creative work with others thereby to serve the common good. While he was an idea man and an encouraging speaker, Swann's ratio of action to talk was high. He was willing to start things himself, beginning where he was.

Swann and his contemporaries — the decentralist intellectuals and activists who shared his commitment to fostering peace, civil rights and community — were in that rebel minority that regards resisting absentee authority as a sacred duty. This perennial resistance probably dates back to the same time that far-off authority started to command its scribes to do recruitment and public relations on behalf of mergers and acquisitions conducted at sword point.

Bob Swann was a natural anarchist, although given the stigma attaching to anarchism, referring to him as a decentralist may better serve his cause. He had an awakened conscience and an existential determination to follow it. By extension he had enough faith in the good sense and goodwill of the average person to believe that their freedom of conscience was vital to the intelligence of a healthy community. Swann was able to differ peaceably.

Although Gandhi pointed the way, Swann's decentralism — and radical pacifism — found American roots and expression. Gandhi humbly titled his autobiography *My Experiments with Truth*. Bob Swann and his contemporaries were less philosophically tentative. Rather than experiments there were actions and projects in architecture, economics, education and homesteading. They took to heart Gandhi's precept that it was not enough to put one's body on the line to oppose injustice — be it colonialism, war, conscription, racism or economic inequity. It was even more necessary to put one's body, mind and spirit into the particulars of developing a nonviolent society from the grass roots up. Nonviolent resistance and constructive program were two sides of one coin for Gandhians.

As did Gandhi, Swann set his mind on the segments of society that are the salt of the earth: small farmers and merchants, mechanics and craftspeople and residents of inner city neighborhoods, rural areas and small towns. He concerned himself with agricultural credit, secure land tenure, equity in enterprise through worker ownership and cooperation; with community-backed credit for local production and with local currencies. Over the 40 years he spent studying, shaping and starting self-help economic institutions, Bob aimed at fortifying community economies to withstand the heedless vagaries of nation-state policy. Participation in the local economy, Swann understood, can be a kind of citizenship that's deeper than politics.

Whatever their avowed ideals or codes, economic and political institutions beyond a certain scale become overly complicated, brittle and clumsy, if not outright exploitive. The logic of decentralism is to find the scale at which the wholeness of conscience, of community and of the land's providence can be maintained. Deeper than politics, deeper than party or propaganda, deeper and more integral than ideology and utopianism, decentralism prizes freedom, responsibility and loyalty to place.

Consider afresh the savvy and agility of the small. A region's economy is like a nervous system for responding to environmental fluctuations and balancing the organism's metabolism. When the scale is right for self-reliance, the economy's intelligence is supple. The global economy, however, is like the coarse, ropy nerve trunks of a wide-ranging omnivore, a hybrid *Brontosaurus rex* — an organism so huge, voracious and lumbering, so much more brawn than brain, that it cannot perceive and respond to the ground-level details that comprise the health of bioregions.

Regulating a leviathan is complicated. At global or national scale, regulation often constrains the regulators better than the prospective regulatees. In the small community, however, people are known to one another and word gets around. It becomes more feasible to bring moral pressure to bear on exploitive bosses, shoddy craftspeople or lazy hands. More importantly, community members can support good enterprises with their participation, their patronage and their savings. And if small-scale decentralized economies fall short of those hopes, their failures need not bring down a whole system.

"No one is coming to rescue you" is a tough-love saying. Harsh though that reminder may be, and certainly not the whole truth, there's a grain of truth in it. It's a counsel of self-help, a prudent recommendation to strive for balance and a measure of autonomy. It pertains to political economy. Worse than no one coming to the rescue might be the conditional mercy of some monolithic rescuing entity from on high.

If centralized monetary and financial systems, and hoarding and trafficking in land spawn conflicts and aggravate inequality, unemployment and exhaustion of natural systems, then why not project a myriad of nonviolent, non-confrontational alternatives to the arrangements that benefit the few and impoverish the many? Why not work at the scale of the possible and develop arrangements conducive to just proportion, individual dignity and shared sufficiency?

It may be that Bob Swann was able to envision the alternatives that he did because he was free of the desire for possession. He was unafraid of poverty. Swann and his spouses lived simply and found fulfillment in doing rather than in having. Swann's innate courtesy and good humor buttressed his courage and his work, as did his affiliation with two remarkably powerful, supportive women. His philosophical bent, fine mind, a great body and a natural enthusiasm kept him free. Not only was he physically capable (a strong worker all his life), his belonging to various intentional communities, cooperatives and affinity groups provided him with a sense of security that was of a different ilk than money in the bank. Community, for all its trials, is the only source of security that most mortals ever know. Moths and rust devour the hoards, but mutual aid, like sunshine, may sustain us from day to day.

For individuals to live freely in community, to obtain a decent subsistence and to follow the dictates of conscience requires moral understanding, meaningful education and fair access to the means of production. When it has been possible, such communal self-management has involved a customary, rather than a pecuniary, relationship to place. What we now know as economics used to be culture. Devolution of economic activity to a sensible scale, like the bioregion, might hold the potential to make economics intelligible, subordinate to the whole life of the community and careful of the land. It could serve to realign our lifeways with more anciently tested patterns.

The majority of human experience has consisted of getting subsistence directly from the land; until fairly recently the exchange of goods and services was minimal, ordained by kin or clan or governed by custom. Markets were peripheral and contained. However in the West, with the enclosure of the commons and the legitimation of the profit motive, a historical divide gaped between vernacular and commercial economies to the ultimate disadvantage of the former. With "the great transformation," so termed by the historian Karl Polanyi,[3] the emergence of the market system meant that commerce, banking and finance began to reshape the world.

Although we talk about them familiarly, global finance and economics, now so fragile and menacing, are arcane. Earlier on, the subject was candidly identified as Political Economy, acknowledging that it was about power relations. Academicians claim that economics is a science, that there are laws of economics as sure as there are laws of physics. If this is so, then rather than being actors and shapers of economies, people and societies are hapless subjects. But history shows that economic "law" has in fact been shaped by intentions, by values.

The ideas claiming to be laws of economics are dictates more than discoveries. They exclude ecology and altruism from their calculus, disregard qualities and fetishize quantities. In conventional economic discourse the benefits of globalization, comparative advantage, economies of scale and continuing growth are assumed. Even as an epochal economic and ecological crisis unfolds, captains of industry, heads of state, ministers of finance and most of the punditry appear to expect those same old assumptions to produce different kinds of outcomes.

Perhaps because he was a self-taught outsider who was interested in the subject for the sake of the common person, Bob Swann's work helped demystify and rescale economic practice and to develop a Third Way in economics. Never content with mere proposition, Swann mounted projects which generally invited and structured popular participation. Swann's ideas brought local community investors, producers and consumers into convivial relationships with one another on the human scale. Bob Swann's thinking was not quixotic. In his efforts to see how new institutions could help communities and regions to involve their people in local production for local needs, he adapted ideas that worked. This is something other than instituting a welfare state.

All his adult life, Bob Swann was a builder and contractor. Bob Swann both thought and led, balancing headwork with bread work until he was too old to swing a hammer. That balance kept his economic thinking useful, close to the ground. He enjoyed physical work and made necessary things like houses. In the circumstances of the near future, where cheap energy is apt to be a bittersweet memory, solar, wind and muscle power may be the most plentiful and least climate-changing energy sources. Skills in making necessary things are likely to be of more value to communities than *haute* finance or downward trickles.

When, in the early 1990s, I first met and briefly worked with Bob Swann and Susan Witt at the E. F. Schumacher Society, I had been aware of Swann's work in community economics through my involvement with bioregionalism. In her *Economics as if the Earth Really Mattered*,[4] Susan Meeker-Lowry catalogued the practices of bioregional economics, highlighting Bob Swann's ideas.

The bioregionalist critique was that industrial civilization and nation-state geopolitics are ecologically obtuse and do violence to the organic complexity of Earth's life-places. The bioregional movement, as the name suggests, regarded the land's character

Bob Swann and Susan Witt

and biodiversity as paramount information, the essential directions for living in place. We would decentralize to our bioregions. The bioregional ethos is recognition and restoration of native landscapes and natural systems. Bioregionalists envisioned and in some places began to develop watershed political economies based on renewable flows of energy and matter. In this we were charting afresh the terrains of consciousness surveyed in the first part of the 20th century by the regional planning movement. Those regionalists, Lewis Mumford most notably, had influenced Bob Swann from his prison reading onwards.

Back when we met, Bob and Susan were busy developing and diversifying the Community Land Trust in the Southern Berkshires, as well as tending and launching several Schumacher Society programs. Swann and Witt were further implementing the ways and means to bioregionalize economics, minus ecological rhetoric. Bob was corresponding with his colleagues in alternative economics around the world. He was advising various groups on the workings of local currencies and looking for funding for the Land Trust's low cost housing project which he had designed and built. In his spare time he was playing tennis with his architect friend Joe Wasserman. I did some writing about the Schumacher Society's work, not entirely comprehending its significance but taking that on faith. Ecology, not economics, was my passion.

It was only later that I learned about Bob's conscientious objection and stint in federal prison. Although I quite appreciated Bob's economic fluency and inventiveness, it was his daring stand as a conscientious objector (CO) in World War II that riveted my attention. Not only had he been arrested, he'd done time.

During the Depression, hard times all round had begged the question of what to do and how to better the world. Living on slender means, Bob Swann found his purpose and an inalienable freedom. Swann came of age in a period that had its own apocalyptic portents: Nazism, Stalinism and a World War featuring the debut of a weapon of mass destruction to beggar the worst imaginings. After protesting conscription and war in a fashion that would more than once land him in prison Bob turned to community economics as a way to better serve humanity. The kind of conviction it took to resist the draft in the 1940s was the kind of conviction it took to labor away in a small nonprofit organization on an economics of peace. When we were talking together in 2001, Bob Swann, then in his early 80s, remained hopeful if not optimistic, alive to the work of implementing the kinds of small changes that could, acre by acre and town by town, help redeem the world.

During the interviews for this book, Bob reminisced about peace actions, international journeys and meetings with remarkable women and men. Because I was fascinated by the courage required for the kind of dramatic civil disobedience Bob had engaged in, I studied the man and kept trying to winkle out the secret of his uncommon ability to cleave to principle. There was no secret as far as Bob was concerned. Among the many morals of this story is that you don't have to be a saint or a genius to maintain your integrity. Of his life, Bob said "It's been fun." What to me looked like sacrifice was catnip to him.

This writing culminates at a moment when the planetary situation looks dire. Climate change, the extinction crisis, the sunset of the fossil fuels era, food riots, water shortages and a dramatic rearrangement of international power relations are all upon us. Regionalism, decentralism, bioregionalism and what's now being called relocalization all have called for a radical reconsideration of our current arrangements and advocated working together in our locales to develop an array of living societies. The small, geographic community is where the real economy still lives, its redoubt when the casinos go bust and it's time to barter and truck.

The daily work has to be performed, regardless. Chop wood, carry water, say the Zen Buddhists. The means to moral, useful local economies are simple, but not easy. Bob Swann and other proponents of right-sized, participatory, self-help economics have given us crucial tools.

CHAPTER 2

The Forging
of His Conscience

W HILE HIS CHILDHOOD was in certain respects idyllic, Bob Swann, born in 1918, grew up in an era when specula-tion and monopoly nearly destroyed the United States. He lived on into an era when globalization, unrestrained trade, fatuous currency, itinerant capital and high-rolling finance were in vogue, their effects amplified grotesquely by the technologies of the post-war era.

Bob Swann was the first of two sons in a prosperous middle class family. Bob's father Clarence Scott Swann was the vice presi-dent of a large printing company. Clarence Swann, said Bob's younger brother Jim, had been a sickly child who, while bedridden, passed the time reading about the "Baron Kings" — captains of industry and heroes of cap-italism. He was, said Jim, "wed to the Republican side." Their mother, Alene, was a homemaker. Alene Abrams had been raised on a farm and, on account of her father being a drinker, had as-sumed the responsibility of running

James and Robert Swann

17

the household she grew up in.[1] Clarence Swann was about 20
years older than the 18-year-old Alene when they married.

"One of her sisters once described…[Alene] as a 'go-go' girl,
full of life and fun and a liking for a good time," wrote Marjorie
Swann Edwin, Bob Swann's former wife. "Bob's father was already an up-and-coming businessman, quite serious, and as Bob
always described him, 'a Taft Republican' — meaning that he was
conservative in his political and social outlook but also honest and
moral…."[2]

The family lived in Cleveland Heights, Ohio. Bob remembered
his neighborhood and the life the parents there created for their
children as "exceptional." There were block parties on special days
like the Fourth of July, with everyone — from adults to the youngest child — participating in their own Sycamore Street parade, ice
cream social and "all kinds of races and games."[3]

Quite as important as the conviviality of the neighborhood
was its setting. "One of the early influences on my life and thinking,"
wrote Bob, "was the accidental design of…Sycamore Street…a
dead-end street with houses built close together…opening to
a hardwood forest where we could play and explore for days on
end."[4] The Sycamore Street neighborhood as a whole was such a
formative influence that it supplied Bob in old age with the kinds
of pleasant memories usually associated with happy families. In
a paper he wrote for a correspondence course that he took while
he was in prison for draft resistance young Bob Swann examined
what growing up there had imparted to him. Early on he intuited
that community consists in more than social relations. It has a
structural, physical dimension and a necessary relationship with
nature.

> When I was but two years of age my parents moved to the
> city of Cleveland. After moving once or twice within the city
> they settled down on a short street in Cleveland Heights, a
> small, undeveloped suburb at the time. Here on this same

street we lived for fifteen years. This was where my experience with a small community began. When we moved there our street contained only a few houses besides ours and these had only recently been built. The street itself was only five hundred yards long unpaved and dead end; it ran into a woods of perhaps ten or fifteen acres. Due, perhaps, to the relative seclusion and rural nature of this street, and to the fact of its recent development, a sense of "pioneering" developed from the very start. The families who were thrown together here developed the pioneering spirit of cooperation, and the sense of mutual community responsibility. By the time I was old enough to be aware of things, I was already conscious of myself as a member of a community larger in scope than the family group. As kids all of us on the street played together constantly. We developed a strong sense of rivalry as well as camaraderie. In our fortunate situation where traffic was scarce, the street itself became our playground for baseball, football, hide-and-seek, diversion and common activity.

Moreover, the woods at the far end of the street was a haven for us against the encroaching aridity of the city — of the automobile and the trolley car. In the woods we could commune in solitude and feel ourselves to be a part of a larger and still unknown universe. The woods, too, were a source of other diversions: in winter there were hills for coasting. The snow took excellent footprints for a fox and hound hunt. There, too, we could practice forms of woodcraft — building fires, building cabins or huts, playing Indian, or collecting wild flowers, and, of course, having picnics and wiener roasts. We used to haunt the woods. Occasionally when the loneliness and "spookiness" of the woods at night especially would frighten us we could come running back home to the security and safety of the community. Then it was, I think that we realized how secure and safe our community was, and how glad we were to get back to its sanctuary. Living though we did in the twentieth century (1920s) and within the area of a large city, we experienced something of the feeling the pioneer must have had about his community. We had a definite sense of "belonging."[5]

School was a less happy feature of his childhood. Although Bob had enjoyed kindergarten, the dull pedagogical regime of the first grade was an unwelcome change. "We all had to sit in our chairs most of the day and listen to the teacher talk," he explained.[6] Bright young Bob could do the schoolwork more quickly than the other kids. To keep himself amused, he would tease a classmate.

"When this activity began to cause a commotion, the teacher reprimanded me.... But one day I apparently persisted and in desperation she tried to catch hold of me. A chase ensued, with all the kids laughing. I managed to get behind an old upright piano where she couldn't reach me. She left the room muttering and returned with the principal. Between the two of them, they managed to pull me out from behind the piano."[7]

The upshot of this precocious anti-authoritarian's mischief was a draconian sentence, arrived at in consultation with Clarence Swann. For two weeks at school Bob was to be locked in a coat closet all day with nothing to do or see. After school he was to go home to his room and remain there until the following day. This is how Bob came by his formative childhood trauma in the first grade: at the hands of a punitive schoolteacher whose severity was abetted by his father's. It may not have been an unusual punishment in its day, but it left an indelible mark on Bob's psyche, a lasting detachment.[8] He remembered his mother trying to ameliorate the house arrest.

I am sure my mother felt very bad about this and she spent a lot of time reading stories to me...while I stayed in my room. I could forgive her but not my father. From that time on I was alienated from my father.... Afterwards, I'm sure I never felt as close to her.[9]

Spending formative time in a forest matrix left a deep impression on Bob Swann. His metaphors for social change would be evolutionary and organic rather than mechanistic. He would sustain a lifelong interest in trees and tree crops. His lifelong agrarianism was fostered early on as well.

Bob spent his eighth and ninth summers on an uncle's Ohio farm. There he learned to work with a team of horses, plowing, raking hay and pulling the hay wagon. He milked the cows morning and night. Unlike so many Americans of his generation he would never forsake his appreciation for agrarian life and all that it meant — from the care of the soil to the teachings of the beasts.

> I loved working with the horses, who didn't need much direction. They knew when to turn at the end of the furrow and where to go when my uncle said "go home".... I liked the way the animals disciplined all of us — they knew when to come home to wait for their bundle of hay and to be milked.[10]

Another childhood experience which Bob thought had shaped him was a Civil War legacy. One of Bob's grandfathers was a Union veteran of the Civil War who had fought with General Philip Sheridan.[11] Perhaps because of this, Clarence "had a collection of daguerreotype photos from the Civil War…a well-known collection by a famous photographer. He kept these large, very realistic photos depicting the dead and dying men of the Civil War stored on the third floor of our house," wrote Bob. "I used to sneak up the stairs to look at them — not that they were a secret, but somehow I felt guilty looking at them. I'm sure that on a subconscious level these photos played a role in my later anti-war convictions."[12] Jim Swann thought that "It was a great rainy day occupation to look at that Civil War book."[13]

Bob Swann grew up during the Bull Market that eventuated in the Great Depression. His youth was a time when much of the world's economy convulsed. He attained manhood amid the ruinous consequences of the stock market crash — the unemployment, the foreclosures and the internal refugee movements, from itinerant hoboes to westering Okies. This, perhaps, predisposed Bob Swann's mind to ponder economic systems and their life-and-death consequences. "The Depression woke me up," he said, "like a big kick in the pants."[14]

His family had been quite prosperous before the crash. When the financial bubble of the 1920s burst they experienced a sharp decline in their standard of living. The Clarence Swanns were never destitute, but their lives were seriously affected. When Bob's father lost his executive position, Alene had to give up her maid and do all her own housework. Although in comparison to losing one's farm or home to foreclosure, or even one's children to malnutrition, this loss sounds slight the ratcheting down in status was distressing.

"We were a reasonably happy middle-class family until 1929," Bob wrote in his autobiography. "Then came the stock market crash and everything changed. My father lost his job.... I remember my mother crying uncontrollably at our loss of income...I was 11 years old.... I felt helpless to do anything about it."[15]

Times were hard, but timeless goods, like art and learning, offered their sustenance. By the time he was in high school, Bob had the good fortune to have the friendship of "a true teacher...Joseph Sittler, who was minister of our local Lutheran church.... I would stop off at his office after school to discuss books he suggested.... I read German philosophers like Hegel, Nietzsche and Spengler, and classical novels like Dostoevsky and Tolstoy.... He also taught me to love classical music, particularly Bach...."[16]

This relationship may have ameliorated the vacancy in Bob's life left by his alienation from his father. "Bob and my dad used to argue tremendously," Jim recalled. "I knew it would never end on a clean note."[17]

Sittler had taken his bachelor's degree in Biology.[18] He served as pastor of the Messiah Lutheran Church in Cleveland Heights from 1930 to 1943. He would leave the ministry in early 1943 to teach systematic theology at the Chicago Lutheran Theological Seminary.[19] By mid-century Sittler would become an outrider of eco-theology, rocking Protestantism with his call to see nature as continuous with God.

When Sittler, in his late 20s, befriended the teen-aged Bob, he may well have been working on a first publication, "A Parable of the Soils."[20] Thoughtful people in those days did concern themselves, for reasons contemporary and historic, with the fate of the soil. The 1930s, of course, was the era of the Dust Bowl as well as the Depression. The Roosevelt administration created a Soil Conservation Service. Yet to sermonize about it with both biological and theological understanding surely was innovative. Although Bob doesn't mention it in his recollections, it seems possible that Joseph Sittler, along with opening the realms of literature and classical music to his gifted young friend, affirmed and encouraged the reverence for organic life and its processes that would inform Bob's thinking from then on. It is tempting to speculate that Joseph Sittler's conviction of God's grace as being immanent in nature helped foster the vitalism that throbs in Swann's early prose.

The relationship with Sittler, however, would wane on serious political grounds. "As the Nazis took over in Germany, Bob was surprised and considerably horrified to discover that Joe leaned toward approval of Hitler," wrote Marjorie Swann Edwin. "By middle teenage Bob had read enough to know that he definitely did not approve of Hitler and the Nazis, and his relationship with Joe cooled."[21]

Living through the Depression left its mark on most of a generation. One could hardly help but notice that conventional economic wisdom was provisional, that Wall Street and the banks might not be the trustworthiest stewards of the country's wealth and that speculation could be a ruinous pastime. Yet as we have seen in the early days of the 21st century the longing to forget those lessons has been immense.

Most people in the US who were born after the 1930s, or whose families dodged the worst of it as both my parents' families did, have been unwilling or afraid to imagine what it is like to have the bottom drop out — to be out of work, unable to pay the bills, unable to feed the kids and to be cold, hungry and out of hope. But if there was desperation there was also solidarity. Reminiscing about the Depression in one of our interviews Bob said, "It was a great time in one sense because everybody said, 'well, we're in the same boat, let's help out.'"[22]

While most of what we know today of the 1930s has to do with Roosevelt and the New Deal, there was in fact a great deal of grass-roots organizing of local economies. People's historian Howard Zinn has written that "By the end of 1932, there were 330 self-help organizations in thirty-seven states, with over 300,000 members." Their efforts to obtain and distribute some of the basic necessities like milk, suggests Zinn, were overwhelmed. "By early 1933, they seem to have collapsed; they were attempting too big a job in an economy that was more and more a shambles."[23] If there were valiant — and sometimes militant — popular responses to the grueling conditions many endured, and some humane initiatives from Washington, the Depression was, finally, a trauma whose lessons Americans denied to their peril.

In the neighborhood where I grew up lived a blue-collar family whose matriarch had weathered the Depression in Appalachia. She'd learned the contradictions between economic theory and financial practice during hard times. Evidently her confidence in banks had been completely undermined. After she died her husband began finding cash that she had stashed throughout the house in books and dressers. It finally totaled about $40,000. She hadn't invested or deposited it. She had been willing to forgo the interest it might have earned in order to have her money within reach.

The Swann family's reduced circumstances meant there wasn't enough money for Swann to enroll in Ohio State University, but in 1935 he went anyway and audited classes. He lived for a couple of years with his father's sister Mary and her husband, a successful lawyer. Bob took and was dissatisfied with the Economics 101 course. "It hit me hard that there was all this unemployment," he recalled. The economics professor, a New Dealer, "didn't know himself what was going on.... 'Monetary economics is not my business,'" said the professor. "From that point on," said Bob, "I kept asking questions."[24]

Bob's passion at that time wasn't economics, though, but the study of art. To support himself Bob did some odd jobs, like being a DJ and selling mops door to door. During his third and final year at the University he lived on the cheap with a bunch of young fans of George Bernard Shaw, the prolific Nobel Prize-winning dramatist and critic. These resourceful free-thinking lads managed to subsist mainly on oatmeal. "While I was at Ohio State," Swann wrote, "I became part of a small student group of 'dissidents.' The half-dozen of us came together because of our similar anti-war beliefs and perhaps because of our creative leanings.... Some of us lived together in a loft above a local saloon." It was not a garret as such, but a bohemian outpost in the midst of Ohio. "Three of us were painters and one of us was the philosopher 'in residence.' We also had one non-resident guru who was a theosophist...steeped in Hindu and Indian philosophy."[25]

Around the time of Bob's 83rd birthday in early 2001, just as we were beginning our interviews, we went out for lunch one afternoon. As the sandwiches arrived, Bob, unexpectedly and untape-recorded, began to rhapsodize on his love of art. He spoke of all the drawing and painting he did in his younger days. He spoke of charcoal sketching and of how quickly one could work in that medium. He remembered his drawing instructor at Ohio State, Hoyt Sherman, a renowned educator.

Hoyt Sherman taught classes at the University's School of Fine Arts. His "innovative and eccentric drawing course…was offered not only to art, architecture and engineering students but also to athletes, dentists and military personnel, all of whom stood to benefit from improvements in their ways of seeing. Sherman's teachings were based on psychological and physical studies of how the mind and eye perceive objects…."[26] Sherman venerated Cezanne, and Bob Swann followed him in that.

"Cezanne was a very intellectual painter," said Bob that day at lunch. In order to really grasp what he, or any great artist was up to, well, he said, you have to spend an hour at least looking at a painting. "You have to forget yourself," he said, "work at it long enough." Bob went on to explain that "What moved me to architecture and building was that it could be beautiful," and credited Hoyt Sherman with turning him on to Frank Lloyd Wright.[27]

When it came time to leave the University, Bob's thoughts turned to farming and to an investigation of pacifism as well. Alex King, a Mennonite friend and fellow dissident, came from a 100-acre family farm near the area where Bob's uncle Alvie had farmed. "I wanted to find out more about all the angles of peace work or peace people. So I asked him if I could come and live with him and his family for a year in Ohio."[28] The two young men worked together, and as he had as a boy, Bob thrived in agrarian life.

> I liked the Mennonite way of life for the same reasons I liked my uncle's farm when I was a kid. I was rejecting the urban way of life for its sterility…. At the same time I wanted to belong to a group or community in which people worked together for the common good….[29]

Near the King farm Bob attended a talk at a Civilian Public Service (CPS) camp and there he met Bayard Rustin. Rustin was a phenomenally gifted black Quaker and war resister who, in 1941, became a youth secretary for the Fellowship of Reconciliation and a protégé of A.J. Muste, the dean of American pacifists.[30] Bob would come to regard Rustin as "probably the most astute organizer of nonviolent direct action in the United States at any time."[31] A persuasive orator, Rustin possessed a beautiful singing voice which he also employed in his campaigning. Rustin's argument for total resistance to conscription "more than anything else" influenced Bob's decision to take an absolute position of noncompliance with the Selective Service System's policy for conscientious objectors.

"Although I was a conscientious objector," he said, "even more fundamental...was my unwillingness to support a draft or conscription system."[32] Swann not only objected to armed service, he objected to conscription per se and so would not consent to do alternative service in a CPS camp. "I was not going to let myself be taken," he said in one of our interviews. "Nobody was going to tell me what I was going to do."[33]

In the spring of 1942, after his year on the King farm, Bob received an invitation from another dissident friend to join in setting up an intentional community. "Without hesitation" he accepted and headed towards Bennington, Vermont. During his brief time there, doing what would later be called organic farming, he was able to visit Scott and Helen Nearing at their farm in Jamaica, Vermont to see for himself how they were faring.[34] The Nearings were a Tolstoyan socialist couple whose 1932 move back to the land and homestead self-sufficiency[35] would — chronicled by them in 1954 as *Living the Good Life* — make them models for generations of hands-on idealists.[36]

Also while he was in New England, Bob met the influential author Richard Gregg at a nonviolence workshop. Gregg was farming on land owned by the Nearings.[37] Bob wrote that this meeting was his "first real contact with the intellectual ideas behind nonviolence and with others who were also seeking alternatives to violence." Swann had by then read Gregg's *The Power of*

Nonviolence (of which more later). The subject he wound up discussing with Gregg, though (and would later correspond on) was organic farming.[38]

It's in keeping that Bob, who really loved physical work — from the agricultural labor he did as a boy on his uncle's farm in Ohio to the construction and contracting he did for both bread and satisfaction until he was 80 — was on an organic farm when the federal marshals came after him. He had written his draft board to inform them that he was unavailable for conscription, and their response was to order his arrest.[39] It epitomizes Bob the Gandhian: learning as a college dropout in 1942 how to restore soil fertility, grow food and live the good and simple life and then risking prison rather than conceding the state's claim to the right to force him to kill.

Joseph Sittler had long before sensitized Bob to literature. As a passionate individualistic young man Bob sought and found the art and literature that sustained him. Thus shortly after he was incarcerated he wrote his brother that for a Christmas present, "the book I would like most, as you may guess, is *Collected Poems and Plays of Rabindranath Tagore*."[40]

Tagore and Bernard Shaw were, in the springtime of Bob Swann's life, the two best-known writers in the world. One of the great litterateurs and educators of the 20th century, Tagore composed songs, poetry and verse plays. Although his *oeuvre* was quintessentially Bengali and his songs are sung in his homeland to this day, even translations (his own, to English, among them) revealed a vast, resplendent wholeness of beauty to the West. Along with his educational endeavors to mingle the respective cultural geniuses of West and East, Tagore's writing earned him a Nobel Prize for Literature.

As we will see, Gandhi and his campaigns of nonviolent direct action to end the British rule of India were a tremendous inspiration to Swann's generation of pacifists. Tagore, Gandhi's contemporary, argued against nationalism itself. He held perhaps a more nuanced, welcoming attitude towards modernity than the village-focused Gandhi and addressed not only Indian but world affairs. On the cause of Indian nationalism Tagore would argue with Gandhi, whom he esteemed highly enough to dub the Mahatma ("Great Soul"). In turn, Gandhi respectfully called Tagore "The Great Sentinel."

By nonviolent noncooperation Gandhi aimed to invite the British to leave India. One tactic was a boycott of British cotton cloth, a product whose manufacture England had usurped from India over the centuries of colonization. To supplant the colonizer's trade goods, the Mahatma urged that every Indian should use the *charka*, a hand spinning wheel, to make cotton thread and then proudly wear the *swadeshi* cloth woven from it. Tagore had his reservations. "Poems I can spin, Gandhiji, songs and plays I can spin," wrote Tagore in 1921, "but of your precious cotton what a mess I would make!"[41]

In later years Bob confided to his daughter Carol that he found his existential motive in a sense of human unity.[42] Carol had been quizzing him on matters of heart and soul. Bob told her that Rabindranath Tagore had been the first source of that conviction of our unity. Carol said, "I asked the burning question of the moment which was 'What made him maintain his optimism in the face of so many obstacles?'"

> His answer took me by surprise. He said, 'I know this might seem like a cliché, but it's what I've always felt. We are all one.' This surprised me. I wondered if my Dad had spent too much time in California after all. But this statement was consistent with his love of the great poet Tagore, who was devoted to 'the Divine Nature, the mystical religion of love which everywhere makes its appearance at a certain level of spiritual culture and whose creeds and philosophies are powerless to kill.'[43]

Hence the emergence of a person strongly inner-directed yet permeable to fine influences, a young man whose intellect and conscience were primed by the mentors he found and by the leading literary and philosophic lights of his time and all time. Bob Swann was a convivial soul, happy in companies of kindred mind or shared purpose. Never a conformist, he and thousands of other young pacifists would make the uphill choice to resist the military draft for World War II and thus place themselves in opposition to the prerogatives of the nation-state — but not to the humanity of the world and their countrymen and women.

CHAPTER 3

Satyagraha, American-style

ALTHOUGH PACIFISTS of the Civil War era engaged in a variety of nonviolent actions,[1] the 20th century largely inaugurated the use of nonviolence in widespread social struggles against various forms of perceived oppression, from gender discrimination, colonialism and racism to the use of force by the nation-state. In the 1940s, conscientious objectors like Bob Swann committed civil disobedience in resisting the draft. In the 1950s to protest the Armageddon insanity of the nuclear arms race, postwar peace activists engaged in all kinds of nonviolent direct interventions: they picketed at the Capitol and Pentagon; they demonstrated and held vigils at faraway missile sites, military bases and bombing ranges. In this they were continuing and enlarging the peace activism that flourished prior to and following World War I.

Learning about this long strong history of radical pacifism and active nonviolence in America has been one of the great revelations attached to writing about Bob Swann's life. Peace movement history is obscured, omitted and re-buried as regularly as women's history. Indeed, the two are often coterminous.

For centuries women and men, members of peace churches, free thinkers, feminists, African-Americans and laborers, anarchists, sectarians, young and old — many thousands of Americans — have been willing to sacrifice their freedom, respectability and personal safety to be peace advocates and war resisters. The demonstrators in "free speech zones" today are part of a lineage of freedom of conscience that dates back to the founding of the United States. Would the general view of protest and conscientious objection be more favorable if the persistence of pacifists and their diversity were taught as integral to American history?

Nonviolence is a sublime form of courage. The choice willingly and lovingly to suffer for the sake of obedience to ethical imperatives against killing, or to achieve wider objectives of nonviolent revolutionary change in social relations, remains astonishing.

People born after WWII might find the extent of early to mid-20th century peace activism surprising. World War I had been unpopular, a tough sell. "[T]here were millions who despised the war, had no illusion about it, never forgave Wilson for it and gave it no more outward support than they were compelled to."[2] It took a lot of government propaganda and coercion to create a public consensus for the United States' entry into the hostilities.[3] In those days, conscription was opposed both by secular individuals and by members of the peace churches. As conscientious objectors, Mennonites, for instance, were imprisoned by the thousands and many were brutalized. These outrages provoked reforms that would moderate the treatment of COs during World War II.

It was around the challenge of conscientious objectors as well as their opposition to war that pacifist organizations like the Fellowship of Reconciliation (FOR), the Women's International League for Peace and Freedom and the War Resisters League (WRL) (begun in 1923 by three women when it became evident that the FOR could not relate to nonreligious COs) were founded in the early 20th century.[4] The efforts of such organizations helped develop a small but significant radical antiwar culture in the US between the two world wars.

"The [second world] war followed years of disillusionment with World War I and two decades of antiwar writing and activity in the United States" wrote Larry and Lenna Mae Gara in their introduction to *A Few Small Candles: War Resisters of World War II Tell Their Stories*.[5] Larry Gara, an absolutist war resister, served part of his sentence for draft resistance with Bob Swann in Ashland Federal Correctional Institution. "The prewar era was pretty much an antiwar time," Larry Gara said in a telephone interview. "Schools would have antiwar speakers on Armistice Day. The Gandhian revolution [had] demonstrated other ways of masses of people dealing with conflict."[6]

Reports of Gandhi's tactics brought new impetus to American radical pacifists. In the early years of the 20th century, Gandhi — first in South Africa and then in India — was developing, and rallying hundreds of thousands of followers to, a practice of principled and respectful, nonviolent noncompliance with injustice. Gandhi called this civil disobedience *satyagraha* — holding to truth. *Satyagraha*, obviously, is not a strategy for the faint of heart. Yet it has proven to be an effective strategy that transforms struggles for liberation from being rounds of violence, repression, resentment and revenge into progress towards just accords.

"The thirties was a time when the nonviolent Gandhian movement against the British occupation and rule in India was highly publicized," wrote Dave Dellinger, a radical pacifist CO and contemporary whom Bob likened to Tom Paine.[7] "I was thrilled to know that a creative and powerful nonviolent movement for justice and equality existed in India, even if it had not yet achieved most of its objectives."[8]

The authors of *Power of the People: Active Nonviolence in the United States* make clear that Gandhi's work was a new dawn.

World War II COs had something...going for them that their World War I counterparts lacked: the beginning of a theoretical study of Gandhian nonviolence as a positive force for social change. Gandhi's brand of nonviolence emphasized building decentralized communities grounded in truth, justice, and mutual aid, and encouraged the use

of mass civil disobedience and noncooperation when the
state interfered with the constructive programme.... by the
1940s, pacifists had begun to implement American versions
of Gandhi's program. They started with communities, vari-
ously called colonies or ashrams, and by the end of the war
they had gained more experience with organized direct action techniques.[9]

Along with newsreels and headlines, Richard Gregg's 1934 book
The Power of Nonviolence brought to Americans an objective explanation of Gandhi's campaigns. The book, Bob said, "got a lot
of circulation among peaceniks like me — people who were convinced but like to have a backup."[10] Gregg, a labor lawyer, had traveled to India in 1925 to immerse himself in the culture. He spent
months at Gandhi's Sabarmati ashram as well as at Tagore's Shan-
tiniketan school.[11] In 1928 Gregg returned from India "committed
to discovering and publicizing the meaning of the Mahatma for
the modern world."[12] Over the years Gregg would write several
books propounding different facets of Gandhi's vision for an independent, self-reliant India. Among these other works were *The Big
Idol*,[13] dealing with money and providing an introduction to Silvio
Gesell's demurrage currency, and *Which Way Lies Hope?*[14] which
explained and argued for Gandhi's agrarian approach to India's
development.

The Power of Nonviolence[15] provided vivid firsthand accounts
of *satyagraha* in action. More importantly the book explained the
praxis of nonviolent resistance. Gregg reprinted newspaper accounts of confrontations between Gandhian resisters and British-
commanded troops at saltpans near Bombay. These transpired at
the culmination of the 1930 Salt March, a mass walk to the sea to
gather salt in protest of Britain's imposition of a salt tax. Many
hundreds suffered and a handful died. To see the unarmed march-
ers brutally beaten and not retaliating was gruesome — and amazing. Some, whom Gregg refers to as "the weaklings," turned and

ran. Eventually, though, the troops sickened of what they were doing. This phenomenal display of spiritual courage — and the implementation of a compelling political tactic — cost the British Raj its moral high ground.

In his interpretation, for American readers, of Gandhi's development of nonviolence and civil disobedience into a force that, without arms, could help unseat a viceroy and forge a modern nation on anciently trodden soil, Gregg was showing Westerners a way to fight injustice by defusing wrath and rendering conflict less destructive. Gregg remained an apostle of nonviolence for the rest of his life, helping to shape the US Civil Rights movement from the mid-50s onwards by providing nonviolence training.[16] When, at mid-20th century, Americans beheld nonviolent black civil rights demonstrators in the South neither retaliating nor capitulating when beset by hoodlums, fire hoses, dogs and police they may have been confounded, but they were witnessing homegrown *satyagraha*.

Leading American peace activists, like FOR's A.J. Muste — whose résumé included careers as a minister, union organizer, labor college administrator and Trotskyite, and whom *Time* magazine in 1937 dubbed "America's Number One Pacifist" — and Bayard Rustin were inspired and informed by Gandhi's campaigns. Gregg was not the only radical pacifist who traveled to India to visit and study Gandhi's practices firsthand. At home, US peace activists mobilized to support Gandhi and the nonviolent struggle for India's independence, demonstrating at British consulates and raising funds for the *satyagrahis*. Among such demonstrators was Marj Shaffer, the future Mrs. Robert Swann. Indeed her first of many arrests for civil disobedience, in 1943, resulted from just such a demonstration in Washington, DC.[17]

The upshot of the years of organizing and education by American peace groups and the stirring example of the *satyagrahis*, along with individual insistence on freedom of conscience, was that during World War II nearly 6,000 men like Bob Swann were imprisoned for draft resistance. Another 12,000 served in alternative service projects. The imprisoned war resisters, wrote the Garas, "were not draft dodgers. Their opposition took the form of open resistance, not evasion."[18]

Incarcerating a youthful cohort of radical pacifists provided a setting for seven-days-a-week conferences, tutorials and seminars. "The work camps and prisons that housed conscientious objectors," wrote Joseph Kosek, "became laboratories for developing the nonviolent methods Gregg had described. There the federal government did what the FOR and WRL could not: it concentrated the most dedicated pacifists in the country into groups and gave them a lot of spare time."[19]

These nonviolent prisoners had a goodly power of mind. It took some well-built grey matter to reason one's way into such demanding opposition to the state's presumption. In Ashland Federal Prison, Bob and his peers protested both racial segregation and absurd regimentation.

"Ashland was the model of a police state," wrote another of the Ashland COs, Arthur Dole. "We were controlled by clanging cell doors, whistles, and calls for 'count' (when we were supposed to stand at the doors of our cells). Dressed in blue denims, we marched to meals or recreation. Much depended on the warden, whether he was benevolent or tough. Officers took their cues accordingly; a write-up for a trivial offense could lead to the Hole. Spies or finks would rat on their fellow inmates in return for favors. Tension was always just under the surface."[20]

Remembering his time in prison from a distance of 60 years, Bob didn't dwell much on the hardship of it, although living within a completely authoritarian regime must have been a harsh test. "Going to jail was not as big a deal as most people would think. When people ask, 'What was jail like? How did you feel about it?' I sometimes answer by saying, 'How did you feel when you went to high school?' It's not that much different."

"I tried to get the most out of everything," said Bob in an interview "and to look at everything as an experience. Okay, here you are in this eight by ten room. You can't get out of it; it's locked up. So what do you do there? Well, it's a real challenge."[21] The worst of it, he said, was the endless monotony. Yet for this hale and handsome fellow who followed both his intellectual interests and his conscience with ready energy, who loved farm work, loved being out of doors and doing tangible things, to have his entire world shrunk to the confines of a prison, to be bounded by walls, always to be subject to endless rules, fed mediocre food and allowed out under the open sky for only a brief time daily or to be even more narrowly pent in the individual dungeon of solitary confinement, must have been pretty rough.

In his autobiography, Bob wrote about time in the Hole, and his game efforts to stay sane.

> I suppose if you are a Tibetan monk (I was familiar with Zen), solitary confinement wouldn't feel much like punishment since meditation requires silence. But if you are a moonshiner from the Kentucky hills, it may not be so good. Some men go berserk and beat the walls of their cell until they drop from exhaustion. As for COs like myself, we could find ways to amuse ourselves. I would take the white bread they gave us for meals (I was on a fast for most of the time anyway), wet it, and roll it into balls about the size of golf balls. I let them get hard and used them for games: juggling; mini basketball using a shoe for a basket; bowling on the hard floor, and the like.[22]

Reading the mature reflections on their imprisonment by some of Bob Swann's CO contemporaries along with Bob's own memories, one is struck not just by the COs' decisiveness in refusing the draft and accepting incarceration, but by their principled consistency within the penal institution. They mostly understood that they needed to abide by the general prisoners' mores. They had to do their time. Yet they strove for justice within the institution. They acted, practicing nonviolent resistance behind bars. "Through it all," wrote William Roberts, another prison contemporary of Bob's, "were the protests, fasts, and hunger strikes (usually focused on some prison injustice such as racial segregation), acts of peaceful noncooperation and their inevitable punishments."[23]

A most dramatic instance of Ashland *satyagraha* happened when [Bayard] "Rustin...personally tried to integrate the prison by listening to the radio with some white FOR members. A white inmate objected and began to beat Rustin with a long stick. The other COs attempted to disarm the man, but Rustin ordered them to stop and absorbed the blows without resisting. The bewildered assailant soon ceased his assault, and Rustin's friends considered the incident a victory for nonviolent resistance."[24] In addition to Rustin's individual action, 14 of the Ashland COs, Bob evidently among them, boycotted the segregated dining hall. Two of them were shipped to another prison. The remaining protesters were condemned to solitary confinement and, according to one source, remained there for several months.[25]

"Going to jail or civil disobedience or anything in which you broke a law brought out a greater sense of commitment and community," Bob said. "In prison when you performed a joint project of breaking down the segregation or discrimination, then that added to and strengthened your commitment."[26]

While most of us may be familiar with Gandhi's use of nonviolent resistance, his *constructive programme* which advocated voluntary land redistribution, local production for local needs and voluntary simplicity is less well known. Yet Gandhi's vision of developing a nonviolent, cooperative society community by community is a mainstay of decentralist thought.

World War II COs were an interesting group. Many were Gandhians, and agrarian decentralists. In anticipation of homesteading, and being American, they were interested in technology of an appropriate sort. Back in 1944 Swann and his cohort in Ashland Federal Prison were devouring information on solar architecture (from *Reader's Digest!*), investigating the potential of using rammed-earth construction for low cost housing and reading up on tree crops. A good many of them also were civil rights activists, developing their chops in prison. On the west coast were COs who were poets, like Kenneth Rexroth, and would start new media, as Denny Wilcher and others did with listener-sponsored Pacifica Radio. After editing a publication in a CPS (Civilian Public Service) camp, CO Henry Geiger would found *MANAS*, a weekly newsletter "focused on ethics as found in philosophical and psychological thought and action of thinkers down through the ages with emphasis on recent centuries,"[27] which brought intellectual sustenance to a broad community of peace and ecology activists for 40 years.

It is striking to learn, in the early 21st century, that in the mid-20th century a number of the individuals who were thinking and would go on to act in ways that, if widely adopted, might have spared us the wholesale ecological and economic collapse we now face, were prisoners of conscience. A question leaps to mind: Is the State incompatible with sustainability?

"War is the health of the State," said Randolph Bourne. The state was compelled to imprison absolutist war resisters many, but not all, of whom were so radical that they were up for building a new kind of society: communitarian, materially simple but ingenious, peaceful, inclusive and egalitarian.

CHAPTER 4

Prison – His Monastery and University

D ECENTRALISM is a modern term created with the contrarian prefix *de-*, which means *to do or make the opposite of*. This implies that centralism is the primal condition and that decentralists arrive on the scene to counter centralization and to disperse what has been centralized. Yet it is centralization that is the more recent and less natural social practice and one whose marginal costs, as the archaeologist Joseph Tainter demonstrated in his influential book *The Collapse of Complex Societies*,[1] inevitably exceed any equitably distributed social benefits. The center can only hold at great expense of topsoil, blood and treasure. And the hinterland folk supplying these eventually balk or break down.

Decentralism may be a modern term, but it refers to a mode that was the norm for the greater part of humanity until the Industrial Age began to displace rural life and centralize production. Politically and economically, centralization can be a violent process, usurping widespread diverse, localized (if not necessarily benign) governance and community self-management. Small wonder that so many radical pacifists were decentralists. Yet the fact that decentralism constitutes a body of ideas articulated throughout the Industrial Age by a diverse group of authors — that there is a rich

history of decentralist thinking — may be as much a revelation to
21st century readers as the discovery of the extent of peace activism in the first half of the 20th century.

Coming of age in the 1960s as I did, attending college in the
San Francisco Bay area during the Vietnam War era and winding
up as part of the bioregionalist avant-garde of the ecology movement, I assumed that it was my generation that invented war protest and a critique of industrial civilization. But not only had there
been an antiwar movement and radical pacifism throughout the
20th century, there already existed a confraternity of anarchist and
decentralist thinkers.

Arthur Morgan, these days lamentably little known, was at
the time of his flourishing in the first half of the 20th century cel-
ebrated for both his civil engineering and his work as an educator.
His flood control projects around the country include a system of
dry reservoirs still protecting Dayton, Ohio from floods; he was
the first chair of the Tennessee Valley Authority; he was President
of Antioch College from 1920 until 1936. Wonderful to say, Arthur
Morgan, one of those 20th century decentralist luminaries whom
Bob Swann regarded as "something of a folk hero."[2], became a
preceptor to the imprisoned COs in Ashland and other Federal
prisons. He offered them a correspondence course on the small
community. His curriculum consisted of writings that went with
the grain of human dignity and nature's patterns as well.

In his books on engineering, education, community and uto-
pias, of which *The Small Community*[3] is perhaps best known, Arthur Morgan did, in Henry Geiger's words, "more to articulate the
idea of Community than any other American." Morgan, wrote
Geiger, "came to realize that the decline of moral standards is
closely related to the increasing depersonalization of human relations. He found in his study of small communities, both past and
present, precisely the elements that are typically lacking in the
complex industrialized society of the city — the moral qualities of

'mutual respect, good will, living for and with each other by united effort for common ends.'"[4]

Teachers live for good students, and Morgan was an inveterate educator. Recognizing that the COs were a self-selected, extraordinarily principled group of men, he invited them, by mail, to become his students. Morgan wrote in an open letter

> The men in the CPS camps are intelligent, with sincere and strong convictions. Rarely are there gathered for continued living together a company in which these characteristics are so marked. For these men to be associated for a considerable period without undertaking as a group to make their highest possible contribution to society would be a tragic waste, almost akin to disloyalty…. Men in CPS camps, instead of just passing the time in physical work with incidental study, or even in individual searching of their minds and motives, might also be doing a more difficult and more important job of working out together a common faith and a common way of life….
>
> You are in camp because of one common element in your outlook—objection to military service. That is not a sufficient basis for a common life purpose and commitment. If you are to come to have such a common way, it must be achieved by deliberate and sustained group effort. The result of such achievement could be a fellowship which would be one of the most vital and creative influences in our national life.[5]

Morgan's curriculum aimed at stimulating and educating such group effort. And if the COs and CPS men were, perhaps by their very nature, too fractious to become a fellowship, they would nonetheless be well represented in peace and civil rights activism as well as in the cooperative movement following the war. It was participation in the course that laid the groundwork for Bob

Swann's interest in community-based economic projects. Larry Gara remembered "the [Morgan] course did give us sort of a focus," and evidently took hold of the men's imaginations because, he recalled, "We had a harebrained scheme of dominating Idaho. All the pacifists would move out there and take over the state through elections."[6]

The course consisted of twenty lessons each with a choice of topics for papers. Morgan, at Antioch, required a minimum of one paper a month. Both generous and frugal, Morgan supplied books and also gummed labels "so the same envelopes can be used until worn out."[7]

In addition to a close reading of his book *The Small Community*, Morgan's syllabus for the course required then-current books and pamphlets on rural community, democracy, social organization and government. Reports of the Ohio Farm Bureau's advisory council meetings, works on the cooperative movement, adult education, credit unions and eugenics were on the list. Among the major works assigned, books big enough to undergird a common faith, were Liberty Hyde Bailey's *The Holy Earth*,[8] Lewis Mumford's *The Culture of Cities*[9] and Peter Kropotkin's *Mutual Aid: A Factor of Evolution*.[10] Throughout the course Morgan's own writings and his extensive comments on the papers would sound a bass line of discipline and prudence, as well as a concern for practicality and application.

As an educator who was also an engineer and administrator, Morgan had not only pondered ideas, but led men in groups. His ideal was the small community, but he didn't suppose that the existence of huge industrial and economic systems and their attendant bureaucracies could be wished away. Indeed, as chair of the Tennessee Valley Authority, Morgan planned and helped build an infrastructure for regional economic development from hydroelectric dams to communities planned down to little details like the height of doorways in individual dwellings. The Tennessee Valley was, Morgan said, "the first place in America where we can sit down and design a civilization."[11] That design for a civilization, be it noted, was situated within a region, and regions were the territories of decentralism.

Whatever its limitations, the small community is the socioeconomic form that has until quite recently characterized the vast majority of human experience. Morgan provided a spare but definitive guide to the ways and means of its development in *The Small Community*, discussing the appropriate scale of communities, economic self-reliance, skills banks, the importance and viability of regional planning and provision for community welfare.

Morgan, like Lewis Mumford, was a regionalist. He wrote usefully about the articulation of different functional units of administration, from the small community to the nation as a whole.

> ...[E]ach level of society shall exercise control over subordinate levels, *but only to the extent necessary for the social welfare.* With every stage of social organization all necessary control from above should be combined with all feasible freedom below.... There can be no sharp, predetermined boundaries between social freedom and social discipline, but in such determinations, society must rely on the responsible good will, common sense, and judgment of its members.[12]

Morgan's championing of the small community may have been idealistic but was not utopian or sentimental. He'd sifted through history, sociology and his own working experience to distill a program for the development of communities that would function much in the timeless way of villages, yet be modern. He concluded *The Small Community* with this reflection on the interplay of scale and freedom.

> The genius of democracy is to eliminate compulsion to uniformity, whether that compulsion be physical force or social pressure, and to develop common outlooks and aims by mutual inquiry, mutual interest, and mutual regard. That

process seldom if ever takes place on a large scale. Rapid large-scale changes generally come by ignoring individual variations and by enforcing large-scale uniformities. True democracy results from intimate relations and understanding, with the emergence of common purposes. The community is the natural home of democracy, and it can be the home of tolerance and freedom.[13]

The existence of those virtues in society's members, Morgan believed, was largely a function of the scale and moral quality of their communities. The long road of character formation has to be traveled in community and entails sobriety and self-sacrifice, qualities that may, in a world where resources and energy grow scarcer, have to come to the fore. This passage from Morgan's *The Long Road* is as resonant today as it was when it was uttered in 1936.

> For Americans as a whole, the great need of the coming years in whatever field they may work, is the building of great character, the defining and clarifying of purposes and motives, the development of integrity and open dealing, the increase of self-discipline, the tempering of body and spirit to endure hardship, the growth of courage, the practice of tolerance, the habit of acting for the general good, and the growth of human understanding and of neighborly affection and regard.[14]

Morgan assigned Peter Kropotkin's *Mutual Aid*, the classic statement of nonviolent anarchism. Kropotkin, as much a naturalist as a moralist, argued his case for the natural competence of human and more-than-human communities to attend to the common weal. Morgan also drew the COs' attention to *Fields, Factories and Workshops*,[15] Kropotkin's meticulously documented work on economic decentralization.

Written to refute the Social Darwinism expressed in Thomas Henry Huxley's 1888 essay "The Struggle for Existence," *Mutual*

Aid (which appeared in 1902) is vastly more than a rejoinder. Kropotkin's extensive researches in natural and human history convinced him that cooperation was more powerful an evolutionary force than competition. In his travels in Siberia and Western Asia, Kropotkin had seen instances of mutual aid everywhere in nature. His thesis, "that nature is both inherently moral and the foundation of all human ethics"[16] illuminated intricate cooperation in every order of being, from flocks of birds and hosts of grazers to the elegant organization of the free medieval city-republics.

When faced with human suffering and injustice, or simple necessity, individuals and communities generally spawn ideas for taking care of themselves and making some gesture towards posterity and the hope of the continuance of the common life. Mutual aid, avowed Kropotkin, is not charity but solidarity, taking care of the parts by minding the whole.

It is not love, and not even sympathy (understood in its proper sense) which induces a herd of ruminants or of horses to form a ring in order to resist an attack of wolves; not love which induces wolves to form a pack for hunting; not love which induces kittens or lambs to play, or a dozen of species of young birds to spend their days together in the autumn; and it is neither love nor personal sympathy which induces many thousand fallow-deer scattered over a territory as large as France to form into a score of separate herds, all marching towards a given spot, in order to cross there a river. It is a feeling infinitely wider than love or personal sympathy—an instinct that has been slowly developed among animals and men in the course of an extremely long evolution, and which has taught animals and men alike the force they can borrow from the practice of mutual aid and support, and the joys they can find in social life.

....[I]t is not love and not even sympathy upon which Society is based in mankind. It is the conscience—be it

only at the stage of an instinct — of human solidarity. It is
the unconscious recognition of the force that is borrowed
by each man from the practice of mutual aid; of the close
dependency of every one's happiness upon the happiness of
all; and of the sense of justice, or equity, which brings the
individual to consider the rights of every other individual as
equal to his own.[17]

With texts like *Mutual Aid*, Morgan was teaching not political science or economics, but an integral social philosophy, thinking to
shape a high-minded, communitarian future in the time beyond
the war.

A more current work on the COs' reading list was Lewis Mumford's *The Culture of Cities*, which appeared in 1938. This world historian and cultural critic's work would become a lifelong influence
on Robert Swann. An active regionalist and passionate humanist,
a champion of meaning and taste in the built environment, Lewis
Mumford was a consummate systems thinker. Scathing in his crit-
icism of patterns of enterprise, ownership, design or planning that
in any way sapped or inhibited the life force, he declared at the
outset of his mighty tome "We must erect a cult of life."[18]

Mumford was a Manhattanite who loved cities as they had
been and again might be. He begins *The Culture of Cities* by evok-
ing the ambience and proportion of the walled medieval city. There
was still the reek of dung in the medieval city, Mumford told the
reader, but the countryside was not so distant, nor the gardens so
small that other fragrances wouldn't mingle in the liberating city
air. He, too concerned himself with questions of scale and power
and his preference was for human scale and distributed power:
"Small groups: small classes: small communities: institutions
framed to the human scale, are essential to purposive behavior
in modern society.... we have overlooked the way in which large
units limit opportunity all along the line...."[19]

In *The Culture of Cities*, Mumford proposed redesign not

merely of settlements but of what he termed the *pecuniary economy*. In this passage he struck to the root and raised a call for community landholding.

> The pattern of out right individual land ownership makes it difficult to zone land areas for permanent use that will best accord with the solid needs and interests of the community.... what is important in a sound scheme of land-utilization is not individual ownership but security of tenure: this is what makes possible continuity of use, encourages permanent improvements, permits long range investment of effort. The public control of land for the benefit of the region and the city as a whole is the outstanding problem for modern statesmanship....[20]

Mumford, like Ralph Borsodi, another leading 20th century decentralist, engaged here the problem of property in land. Particularly during the Depression years, the concentration of land ownership and the dispossession of householders and farmers spawned serious consideration, even within the federal government, of redistribution of land.[21]

As exploitation of fossil fuels reaches its maximum, the 21st century will likely see the apogee of metropolitan and suburban sprawl. The causes of this land use pattern are many, but the capitalist relation to land and — in the US — the almost universal dependence on automobiles surely rank high among them. Today's citizen groups struggling to promote the euphemistic, oxymoronic "smart growth" hark back to the regionalist movement of the late 19th and early 20th centuries. Regionalists envisioned urban growth by budding off and reproduction rather than gross expansion, by planning compact, convivial, self-reliant communities dispersed through the countryside with generous expanses of unspoiled land around them.

Reading Mumford exposed Bob Swann to some visionary tenets for shaping the life of settlements. The region would be the middle ground, a sensible territory, neither an imperial power state nor an isolated enclave. Mumford wrote

> In its recognition of the region as a basic configuration in human life; in its acceptance of natural diversities as well as natural associations and uniformities; in its recognition of the region as a permanent sphere of cultural influences and as a center of economic activities as well as an implicit geographic fact — here lies the vital common element in the regionalist movement. So far from being archaic and reactionary, regionalism belongs to the future.[22]

Another lifelong inspiration took hold of Bob Swann during his time in Ashland: Frank Lloyd Wright's architecture. Mumford had extolled it in *The Culture of Cities*, illuminating the social potency of the architect — the person who can design, build and realize the physical basis — the dwelling places of a life-affirming *biotechnic* society. Wright's architecture was both beautiful and iconoclastic. It was, as Mumford recognized, truly novel in being freer of line than anything done before. Rhetorically, if not always functionally, Wright's architecture respected the disciplines of site, budget and materials. In his exploration of the potential of materials newly come to hand and his instinctive reinterpretation of the age-old practice of fashioning dwelling houses harmonious with their settings, Wright aimed at providing common people with worthy, simple and comely homes, proposing the *Usonian* house. From 1948 to 1956 Bob would work in Kalamazoo, Michigan building several of Wright's Usonian houses.[23] The houses that he himself would later design were also Wrightian — modern yet timeless and psychologically sheltering.

Being confined physically didn't stifle Bob Swann's intellectual energy. Some of it found an outlet in his correspondence with his younger and only sibling, Jim, who kept these letters. Despite the constraints imposed by prison censors they make lively reading.

In a September 15, 1942 letter from the Rensselaer county jail, in Troy, New York where Bob was first taken after being arrested, he offered the newly matriculating Jim brotherly advice about getting situated at Ohio State University in Columbus. Then Bob took up the subject of architecture. "Architecture," wrote Bob, "can arise only out of a great oneness of heart and mind. Thus, with a single vision, men work together, to build the living architecture of their joy."[24] By September 30, Bob had been relocated to Columbus, Ohio, perhaps pending his trial for refusal to register for the draft. Mundanities came to the fore and he asked Jim to obtain socks, underwear, a toothbrush and dentifrice for him.[25]

Three months later, Bob was situated in the Ashland Federal Correctional Institution. "[I]t is very reminiscent of our high school," Bob wrote, "except that our confinement is essentially physical not mental." Many of his fellow inmates came "from the mountains of Kentucky," and were, he thought, probably enjoying a higher standard of living in prison than they did at home. Bob said he was becoming accustomed to hillbilly language, songs and humor. He asked Jim to send him Tagore's *Collected Poems and Plays* for a Christmas present, which was the only permissible way he could receive a book. If the Tagore should be out of print, Bob wrote, "I should prefer to have you send my copy of Whitman."[26]

In a subsequent letter, written sometime in December of 1942, Bob reported on a show put on by and for the inmates. "[A] few of the boys in the show were professionals, but most of them were amateurs. It included singing, tap dancing (negro), a couple of clowns, and music by a piano, violin and guitar. I haven't laughed so hard in a long time," he wrote. Bob was also reading St. Exupéry's *Wind, Sand, and Stars* and recommended it to Jim "because the writer is a poet who wanders in the modern world, seeking to understand his fellow men."[27]

After an eight-month hiatus in the correspondence (which may possibly coincide with Bob's time in solitary confinement), Bob wrote to Jim on August 30, 1943. He had turned "intensively to sketching and drawing" and had "discovered an amazing hidden fecundity" within himself. He had made 50 sketches, his best ever, he thought, of horses, cows, bulls and "Women. There seems to be a law of compensation which determines that the imagination compensate for that which is lacking in the immediate everyday experience."[28]

In the next letter to Jim, by then at Clark University, Bob "urgently" requested a book Jim had mentioned reading on Eliel Saarinen's ideas on *organic decentralization* because Bob would shortly begin Arthur Morgan's correspondence course on small communities. "Morgan, himself," Bob wrote, "came down here to arrange the details. The course, itself, is more concerned with social and economic problems of the community including considerable study in cooperatives, but I'm also interested in the physical problems, architectural problems of building a small community...."

In addition to the Saarinen work, Bob also requested a book by Frank Lloyd Wright on architecture. This keen interest in Wright and architecture, Bob explained, arose from "some information... on 'rammed earth' construction...which...Wright is using on his new housing project up in Detroit...which is financed by a group of industrial workers using the co-operative type of business organization."[29]

By January of the next year, Bob wrote to Jim, "*Wright* has arrived!" He was reading Wright and Mumford both and was inspired but sobered by "Wright's constant difficulty" in persuading his clients of the value of his innovations. "Thus," realized Bob, "the new architecture is always awaiting the proper social milieu." And its form will be dependent on its function, which will be quite different under capitalism than, say Scandinavian-style cooperation.

> [A]s Mumford suggests the new architecture will find itself more in harmony with the new emergent social order, one based a great deal more on the concepts of Cooperation,

Decentralism, and Regionalism than on the old and now dying order....

...the main point of it all is that if we are just given a chance we may be entering (after the war) into a period when the old will rapidly fade away and the new will emerge to grow rapidly into the more dominant culture. (I'm speaking in terms of fifty to a hundred years, I realize the next ten to twenty may be perilous.)

But what a chance! I'm beginning to think the architect will be foremost among the leaders of the creative renaissance of the future. If we have one, and I don't see how we can put it off forever. We're overdue now.[30]

Bob and his mates made a serious investigation of the costs and possibilities for building low cost solar housing. His letter to Jim of February 22, 1944 reported on their researches on solar heating, double glazing and various forms of insulation. The men had hopes to work together after their release to establish a *"Nonviolent* training school" à la Gandhi and were "already working on architecture plans for this farm [owned by one of the men, near Columbus, Ohio] as a school and self-sufficient decentralist unit."[31]

The idea of the school-farm continued to engross Bob and his friends throughout the spring. They were so eager to build the world anew when they were free to make the attempt! In an April letter Bob addressed his brother, now in the Army, as "Poor private Jim." He referred to prison as his "monastery" and wondered "if I'll understand what goes on with the world when I get out there." He characterized his prison experience as an opportunity to inquire what life is all about and to place it "on an ever more basic and deepening plane."

The studies continued along with the philosophical inquiry. Bob's mother had obliged his request to send J. Russell Smith's book, *Tree Crops*.[32] "I am growing," he wrote, "continually in the directions of trees on the farm, especially nut trees and timber trees."[33] It is striking to realize that the visions of these COs prefigured initiatives that today are being called *Eco Villages*, *Transition Towns* and *Permaculture*; again, what an extensive history there is behind what we may think are contemporary innovations.

On April 21, 1944, Bob wrote to Jim in a vernal ecstasy: "...Today really was spring. I can't remember when I've felt any better.... Life is amazing, wonderful, more abundant than anything man can imagine. Why...with all the world going mad should life come streaming full, throbbing with an impulse, to lift man with it towards the unending tide of optimism?...Man with his puny wars can no more prevent the onward march of nature than he can stem the tide of the ocean."

It would be interesting to know whether anything other than spring prompted Bob's joyous pantheism. That capacity for enthusiasm would never leave him, though. Part of the prisoner's joy was in having acquired a direction. "I feel unhesitatingly that I know something about where I'm going," he told his brother. "And this in itself is a security beyond all power of words to convey."[34] Through much of his life Bob retained that inner direction and sense of security. They would allow him to live a life in concert with his ideals, quite apart from the suburban materialism of the postwar era.

Bob's organic view of life gave him an evolutionary metaphor for what he hoped would, and in fact did become his life work of building communities. In a May 5, 1944 letter to Jim, he explained the importance he attached "to these seemingly unimportant mutations which I propose to devote my life to bringing to fruition." Integrally conceived communities would be mutations within the whole of society and presumably the catalysts of an organic shift towards human harmony "with these laws of nature, of the universe, of...[man's] own inherent nature." Inspired by Morgan, Wright and Mumford, Bob Swann could imagine a social transformation fostered by the architecture — most broadly conceived — of the small community. He was ready to get to work on it; and he was willing to start "humbly, with a chicken coop, perhaps, and slowly build from there."

By this time in his prison stay, Bob had attracted Morgan's attention and there was discussion of founding a Community Architectural Service, possibly through Morgan's organization, Community Service, Inc. The architectural service would create plans, supervise construction and even devise prefabricated elements to allow unskilled owners to "do their work."[35]

Bob clarified his evolutionary-decentralist social philosophy at greater length in another letter also dated May 5, 1944.

> The need of a world heading in the direction of decentralism…is these small organically planned, integrally built decentralized community units.… [T]hey will be, as Mumford puts it, the delicate plants of the new 'biotechnical era' into which modern civilization is struggling to be born through the pain of war.… [T]hese emergents…are…necessary forerunners.… without them it would be impossible for a truly evolutionary process to go on.… [W]hen any new form such as Socialism, communism, anarchism, cooperation, etc. is attempted by the surgical process (witness Russia!) the inherent laws of biology are violated and…the resultant form is weak and tends toward reaction or atavism.…[36]

Now, this is an expression of faith more than ambition. It is a purely nonviolent imagining of social change, and one which Bob saw as novel, made possible by modern scientific and artistic understanding — a hope to redeem civilization yet.

The remaining letters from Bob to Jim increasingly concerned the technicalities of, and prospects for early parole from his five-year sentence and the possibilities of working in Yellow Springs, Ohio with Arthur Morgan. By August 1944, Bob had learned that the terms of the COs' parole would be restrictive, requiring them to work in tax-supported institutions no closer than 150 miles to home. He told Jim that he had applied for a job at a Child Study

Center in Baltimore Maryland.[37] Bob's dream of working with
Arthur Morgan and launching a Community Architectural Service was deferred.

Nearly 70 years ago the COs in Ashland Prison were designing
decentralized, self-reliant communities and rammed earth, solar-
heated houses. They were finding articles about earthen buildings in *The New Republic* [38] and claims for the efficacy of passive
solar heating via thermo pane windows in *The Reader's Digest*.[39]
Imagine what America would be like today if, when Bob and his
cohorts emerged with such a vision, they had met with encouragement rather than the stigma of being ex-cons — and pacifists at
that. Imagine what life would be like now if rather than redoubling
its militarism and consumerism, the US had taken a turn towards
peace, regionalism, resource conservation and local self-reliance!

CHAPTER 5

Marriage and the Movement

B Y SEPTEMBER OF 1944 after having served two years of his five-year sentence, Bob Swann was released on three years' parole. With a new suit of clothes and $20, he went to Washington, DC, to check in at the Committee on Conscientious Objection, which had been established to monitor the COs' treatment in prison. There he encountered Marjorie Shaffer, a radical pacifist with a talent for leadership and administration, who was effectively directing the office. Having moved from her hometown of Chicago to Washington DC, Shaffer, who was already a veteran activist, "took a leading role in a local union-organizing campaign [and] worked on the cutting edge of the Congress of Racial Equality (CORE)."[1]

Coming from a farm in Iowa, moving with her family to Chicago and looking after the house and her younger siblings while her parents were at work, Marj had become a hard worker early in life. She had had an appalling childhood; her father, a World War I veteran, was violently abusive.[2] Marj's intense determination and her zeal for justice attest a rebel spirit perhaps spurred by her early miseries. Over the years she would show herself to be unafraid to take on the impossible.[3]

Working her way through Northwestern University in a variety of pink-collar jobs, Shaffer was led to pacifism by Ernest

Fremont Tittle, pastor of the First Methodist Church of Evanston[4] who was a Social Gospel proponent concerned with applying Christian principles to the political order. Over the ensuing decades, Shaffer would be active with the American Friends Service Committee (AFSC), Peacemakers, the War Resisters League (WRL), the National Association for the Advancement of Colored People (NAACP), the Fellowship of Reconciliation, (FOR) and CORE, of which she was a charter member.[5] In addition to pacifism, another thing Swann and Shaffer had in common was jail experience, for Shaffer had spent a week in the women's detention center following an arrest outside the British consulate where she was protesting Gandhi's imprisonment.

Bob Swann "was paroled to a job as a 'counselor' at...an institution in Baltimore, where he quickly found out that he had gone from being a prisoner to being a 'screw' — a guard at a penal institution."[6] Shaffer and Swann evidently hit it off, for although he would work for some months at the Child Study Center in Baltimore, he "reluctantly shuttled back and forth between Washington and Baltimore in order to spend as much time as [he] could with Marj."[7]

From the Child Study Center, Swann continued his correspondence with Arthur Morgan, still aiming to work with him. "In my spare time," Bob wrote, "of course, I shall continue to prepare myself for community work, and I am hoping that it will not be too long before parole restrictions will be eased enough that I can come to Yellow Springs."[8] Bob groped for ways to apply what he had learned through Morgan's course to the new confines of his job at what was almost, but not quite, a reform school.

In a letter to Morgan written in November 1944, Bob admitted to having been in a terrible funk.

> I am very sorry to have delayed answering your letter for so long. The main reason has been due to the low mental condition I have been in since release from prison. I have found

this job very taxing on my energies both physically and men-
tally. I had thought, having been in such excellent condition
while in prison, that nothing could get me down, but I have
discovered that something can, and that something is some
twenty kids with extreme emotional and neurotic disturbances. Not having had any experience with children before,
I have found myself all but snowed under. To this deficiency
has been added the difficulties of adjustment to outside conditions after two years in prison.[9]

By March of the following year, Bob had moved to Washington,
DC, where a fellow CO helped him find work at St. Elizabeth's
Hospital. He roomed with two other recently-released COs and
three women, one of them Marjorie Shaffer. Bob wrote Morgan
that his health had improved "100%."[10] On June 23, 1945, Robert
Swann and Marjorie Shaffer were married. Their daughter Barbara, who later took the name Dhyana, was born that November.

In a letter from Philadelphia dated October 27, 1945, the
peripatetic Swann told Morgan that he was married and working at the Friends Neighborhood Guild, still on terms of parole.
He described the Guild as a "Settlement House emerging into
the status of a Community Center" and said, "Here I have an opportunity to explore what some of the possibilities of 'community'
are within the limits of the City." He also mentioned that he had
been helping a local architect build himself a house and expected
to help him with other projects around Philadelphia in months to
come.[11]

In early spring of 1946 the correspondence between Bob Swann
and Arthur Morgan concerned Bob's bid to serve as the executive
secretary of the Miamisburg, Ohio, Community Civic Association, a job for which Morgan had recommended him. Although
Bob was considered an attractive candidate, the stigma of his imprisonment worked him woe and he wasn't hired.[12] Then followed
an exchange of letters trying to figure out a way for Morgan's

organization, Community Service, Inc., to employ Bob and Marj
and to house the newlyweds with their new baby. Morgan was gracious, but working with slender means and trying to strike as good
a bargain as possible, as were the Swanns.[13] Before long, Bob began working for Morgan.

By June of 1946 the Swanns had sent their household effects to
Yellow Springs. A pleasant little college town boasting a great nature preserve (where flows the Yellow Spring) and old-fashioned
neighborhoods notable for their lack of 19th century baronial
mansions, Yellow Springs was described by one old friend of the
Swanns as "a liberal oasis in a conservative to reactionary Midwest."[14]

"Marj, baby Barbara and I left [Philadelphia] to begin a new
life in Yellow Springs working with Morgan," Bob wrote in his autobiography, "My work with Morgan, however, didn't last even a
year. He really needed an administrator to manage the office and
plan conferences, skills which I didn't really have. Marj worked in
the office, too, and was much more useful than I."[15]

Although Bob's employment with Morgan was short-lived, the
Swanns remained in Yellow Springs for a few years. It was there
that Bob learned building and construction, which would be his
bread labor for the rest of his life. After his brief stint at working
for Arthur Morgan, Bob learned carpentry, design and construction. With these skills Bob Swann was able to give tangible expression to his artistic nature.

> What moved me to architecture and building was that it
> could be beautiful.[16] I wanted to construct buildings and
> houses... That was much more my passion than a political
> passion.[17]

February 1948 letters from Bob — who signed himself "Coordinator of the Yellow Springs Housing Association" — addressed to
Arthur Morgan, to a Yellow Springs land owner named Bean, and
to a staff member of the Ohio Farm Bureau detailed a plan for a

low cost cooperative housing project on the outskirts of town. The Association included seven families, eager to have homes. Bob's letter included several examples of successful nonprofit cooperative housing projects around the central US, demonstrating their proven feasibility. The Association, or perhaps Bob on its behalf, had analyzed the pros and cons of two different possible sites and looked to Antioch College and the FHA for possible financing.[18] Evidently despite all the care that went in to the proposal, nothing came of it, for the Swanns would move to Barry County, Michigan the next year.[19]

In his letter to Morgan about the project Bob sounded frustrated.

> "Many worthy projects are lost, given up, or forsaken because of personal interests, personal commitments, or simply false notions.... In this way the community interest is often betrayed.... For real estate, because it is precisely limited in size and total quantity, is a commodity for which the conflict between individual rights and community rights is most acute.... today the pressure of population and the need for careful community planning has brought an increased demand for community interest to take precedence over individual rights and personal interests."[20]

Apparently the landowners did not agree. Still these letters document the beginning of Bob's long career as a contractor, and one whose projects generally involved both social and architectural innovation. Twenty years later, through his innovation of the community land trust, Bob Swann would find some instances in which community interest could take precedence without extinguishing certain individual rights in property.

World War II was over but radical pacifism was not. When the US dropped atomic bombs on Hiroshima and Nagasaki, war became a global death threat. Early pacifist actions against the incorporation of nuclear weaponry in the US arsenal boycotted citywide civil defense drills, characterizing them as preparing the citizenry to accept the practice of atomic war.

Conscription didn't go away either. Although the wartime draft elapsed, by 1947 the Pentagon was pressing for a revival of universal conscription. Conscientious objectors, with their spouses and toddlers, demonstrated their objection to the draft on picket lines,[21] by the first draft-card burning and by draft counseling, which was treated as a crime.

Post World War II peace activism engendered publications and organizations, none more radically nonviolent than Peacemakers, "an anarcho pacifist group."[22] Peacemakers went deeper than politics. A Peacemakers pamphlet proposed that rather than simply to mark a ballot, "the way to vote for peace is to act and live peace." The pamphlet suggested "standing up for the right of anybody to have his say;" opposing "racial or religious discrimination in your neighborhood;" refusing "to be drafted for suicidal atomic and biological war," to make war weapons or to pay taxes for these weapons and going "quietly to work to organize…economic life on the basis of cooperation and mutual aid."[23]

One of Bob's sidekicks in carpentry from Yellow Springs, Ray Olds, was part of Peacemakers too. Olds came to visit Bob in Cameron House on August 24, 2001. I was present with my tablet and my tape recorder during their conversation. The Peacemakers, explained Olds, was "The best support group I've ever been part of…. The Peacemakers was a focal point in our lives."[24]

Marj and Bob Swann were among the originators of the Yellow Springs Peacemakers group as were Wally and Juanita Nelson. Marj had been acquainted with the Nelsons since the founding of CORE in Chicago in 1942. Another of the Yellow Springs Peacemakers (and babysitter for the Swanns) was Coretta Scott, an Antioch student activist who would later marry Martin Luther King, Jr.[25]

Juanita Morrow Nelson had embarked upon a life of direct action as a student at Howard University in 1943. After she and two other coeds were denied service at a lunch counter, she took the lead in a campaign of sit-ins and pickets to remedy the situation.[26] After leaving Howard, Juanita became a journalist and went to work on a weekly newspaper in Cleveland. She co-founded a CORE chapter in that city. Reporting led her to jail to do a story on Wally Nelson, an incarcerated noncompliant CO, an Arkansas sharecropper's son.[27]

Although "CORE used nonviolent tactics," Juanita said, meeting Wally was her first encounter with pacifism as such. The two would become partners for life.[28] Wally Nelson would serve two years in prison and be released after a three and a half month hunger strike protesting penal system injustices.[29] Wally, who'd been active in both labor organizing and civil rights was one of the participants, in the spring of 1947, in the historic Journey of Reconciliation, an interracial effort to integrate travel and accommodations in the South.[30]

Juanita Nelson, wrote Marian Mollin, "recalled being 'hopping mad' about not being able to participate in this pathbreaking project,"[31] which entailed real dangers as the black members of the teams of travelers, among them Bayard Rustin, were harassed and beaten on more than one occasion. Forming community then "became Peacemakers' new strategy of choice."[32] This meant communal living, cooperative projects and pooling resources. In late 1950, the Nelsons and Ernest and Marion Bromley formed a collective household in Gano, Ohio whence they worked on community organizing and integration campaigns.

The Nelsons lived such that their income never reached a level that would be taxable. Juanita was so noncompliant with what she regarded as illegitimate authority that on one occasion, when the Feds came calling to arrest her for nonpayment of taxes and found her in her new white terrycloth bathrobe from Sears, she not only went limp but decided that changing into her street clothes would be a form of compliance. She was carried off to jail wearing only the bathrobe.[33]

In August of 2004, I met and spoke with Juanita Nelson to learn more about Bob Swann, but also about her. Although she is phenomenally courageous and principled, she resists beatification — for the point of being a Peacemaker is that it is just a human way of life, and does not earn one the privilege of pointing the finger at others. Juanita had and has no appetite for sainthood. She and Wally enjoyed their subsistence life in a home they hand built near Deerfield, Massachusetts. It was there that I visited her, finding no electricity, no telephone, no indoor plumbing and water hauled up by hand from the well. Food was grown in a big garden from saved seeds.

The Nelsons, like the Swanns, were leaders of postwar radical pacifism, part of a core of activists that included the redoubtable A. J. Muste, Bayard Rustin, David Dellinger and Catholic Worker movement co-founder Dorothy Day.

Later, during the late 1950s, when Bob Swann was supervising construction for Morris Milgram's open housing project Concord Park, near Philadephia, he would invite Wally and Juanita's participation. And so it was that in addition to her peace work and writing Juanita wound up helping to look after the Swann kids when Marj was famously imprisoned for a symbolic trespass onto a missile base.

In 1949 the Swanns moved to Barry County, Michigan to be near the Circle Pines Center, which had begun as that "embryonic Folk School" Bob had mentioned to Jim. The center descended from a Grant, Michigan Folk School where the Central States Cooperative League would meet. By the late 1940s it was a 284-acre family camp cooperatively owned by scores of members. Circle Pines was also a place where self-organized adult education for social change was as much a part of the ethos as canoeing, tree planting or folk dancing.

Neither capitalist nor communist, cooperatives were a 19th-century social invention for doing necessary business without excessive profiteering or autocratic management. In a cooperative, each member purchases a share of ownership that entitles her or him to one vote and the opportunity to be elected to the governance of the cooperative. Cooperative principles stipulate a limited return on investment. After the members' dividends from the co-op's operation are paid, the remaining profits are reinvested in the co-op's business. Cooperation among cooperatives is also a guiding principle — quite the antithesis of the competition unto death that characterizes capitalism. In contrast to the centralized planning and ownership of state socialism, co-ops are democratically controlled.

Being a Michiganian and a longtime cooperator myself, I've been part of gatherings held at Circle Pines Center whose heart is a pleasant old farmhouse with a meeting room still decorated with murals from its early days depicting a rainbow of hearty folk enjoying happy communal activity. In the summer of 2008 I went there to fossick around in the Circle Pines archives for documentation of the Swanns' doings. Bob's brother Jim, who became an architect, wound up on the Center's staff as builder and with Bill Kernan designed the spare, majestic 36-by-72-foot Recreation Hall. Construction was begun in 1949 and completed by 1956 with a hipped roof that Bob had a hand in designing. "When they tore down an old music hall in [nearby] Hastings," Jim Swann said, "we got the trusses." The brothers oversaw the building of the hall's piers from the abundant local stone.[34]

Circle Pines' first director, Dave Sonquist, was a pillar of the cooperative movement, extolled for his "affectionate liberating leadership." Much admired by both Bob and Jim Swann, Sonquist had been president of the Central States Cooperative League and educational director of the Central Michigan Cooperative Federation.[35] He saw cooperation as a promising way of life that steered between the extremes of anarchism and collectivism.[36] That is, cooperatives are neither right nor left, but an economic and cultural Third Way — and highly participatory. Sonquist's vision was "of cooperation as a way of life in which people can learn how to live together in peace and harmony, with a solid economic foundation."[37] Small wonder that Bob and Marj Swann gravitated to this hive of cooperators who came from throughout the Midwest, quite a few from the south side of Chicago.

As I pored over the early documents in the Circle Pines files — the newsletters, program announcements and correspondence — the vibrancy of the co-op movement of those days became palpable. There was the same air of enthusiasm and hope for better possibilities in the postwar years that Bob Swann had expressed in his letters from prison, a positive spirit of self-help and inventiveness.

Aaron Green, an apprentice to Frank Lloyd Wright, was a member of Circle Pines and led a delegation from the Center to Wright's Wisconsin atelier, Taliesin, to discuss the possibility of having Wright design the Center. Wright did produce a site plan, one rendition of which is in the Center's archives. A futuristic behemoth, it was never executed. Another Circle Piner, Lewis Gosho, was building some Wright-designed houses in Kalamazoo, Michigan and asked Bob to work with him, which prompted the Swanns' move to the vicinity of Circle Pines.[38] Interestingly, and evidence of the interconnectedness of the various decentralist movements in those days, Louise Strandness Gosho, Lewis Gosho's wife, had met Ralph Borsodi (of whom we shall learn more later) and studied community and decentralization at Borsodi's School of Living in the late 1930s. The Goshos bought land adjacent to Circle Pines Center with the aim of starting a homestead there.[39]

The Wright houses were completed in 1954 and, wrote Bob, "there wasn't much work left in the Kalamazoo area."[40] Then a Circle Pines friend asked Bob to design and build a family home in South Chicago. Bob leapt at the chance. The commission gave him an opportunity to work with his brother Jim, but for a time necessitated their commuting from the Kalamazoo vicinity to Chicago.

For a while Bob worked in partnership with Jim on houses around Chicago. The first house that the Swann brothers designed and built together, in 1954, was a prizewinner. "We did a lot of experimenting with it," said Bob[41] of the house which received the *Best Home Design of the Year* award from the Chicago *Sun*.[42]

At the beginning of 1953, shortly after their third child Carol's birth, the Robert Swanns moved to Hyde Park in Chicago where they and the James Swanns and another family lived on three floors in what Marj remembered as "huge apartments."[43] It was a vertical extended family commune, with Bob and Jim working together in Swann Associates, a designing and building business,[44] and Marj doing secretarial work at a PR firm. Meals and childcare were shared among the households. Judy, the Swanns' second child, remembered this home as a spell of 'luxury living,"[45] albeit brief, for the Swanns had a different address in the Chicago suburbs the following year and another the year after that.

In 1956 Morris Milgram asked Bob to come to Philadelphia to supervise construction on Concord Park, a pioneering interracial, or open, housing project. Bob "supervised construction of 59 houses in North Philadelphia and Princeton, New Jersey, homes among the first in the US to be sold to both black and white families by a private builder who made a major breakthrough by obtaining mortgages for integrated housing."[46] An extraordinary developer in many respects, Morris Milgram had once been executive secretary of the Workers Defense League[47] which from the mid-1930s onwards campaigned to "obtain justice for labor organizers, government critics, victims of racial and economic discrimination, and conscientious objectors, through established legal processes."[48] Milgram, a Democratic Socialist, credited Pauli Murray, who had been Juanita Nelson's mentor at Howard University, with motivating his work to increase the availability of low- and modest-cost multiracial housing.[49]

In 1959 at the height of the *Leave it to Beaver, Father Knows Best* era, the Swanns' family life took a dramatic turn. The full complement of four children had been born. Scottie, the youngest, was a toddler. Bob was supervising construction for Milgram. They had a modest family home in Milgram's Concord Park development, on Sussex Road in Trevose, Pennsylvania. Marj combined motherhood with helping Bob administer the construction work, and both Bob and Marj were active with Peacemakers and the Committee for Nonviolent Action (CNVA). As it had the year before, the CNVA organized a project to witness against weapons of mass destruction, this time at an Intercontinental Ballistic Missile base near Omaha, Nebraska. After consulting with her colleagues and family Marj pursued her intention to participate in the Omaha Action, as did A. J. Muste, Brad Lyttle and a dozen or more other CNVAers.

Marj assured everybody that she was going only to support the more assertive actionists. She would just help with administrative details and wash the dishes. Bob along with the two eldest children, Barbara and Judy, figured that with the help of friends and neighbors they would be able to take care of the housework and look after the younger children, Carol and Scottie, for a while. They prepared to cope without Marj for a few weeks.

Judy, Dhyana (then Barbara), Bob, Scott, Marjorie and Carol in 1967/68

Once in Omaha, Marj worked with her usual skill and intensity at organizing and publicizing the action and its purposes, looking for opportunities to argue the case for disarmament and an end to war with any likely group or church that would give the pacifists a hearing. Over the first weeks of the action, several of the activists publicly made the symbolic trespass into the base and were arrested. Marj began to feel a spiritual call to join them and to make the serious sacrifice of her freedom. She fasted and prayed about it. In protracted long distance phone calls Marj discussed her intention with Bob, who knew prison from the inside. He begged her not to do it but in the end respected his wife's decision. In an act of very civil disobedience Marj, dressed in silk, climbed the fence, as did the 75-year old Muste.[50] Marj was escorted out and crossed back in whereupon she was arrested.

In court the judge offered to mitigate her punishment on the condition that she forswear protesting on government property. This she refused to do. The judge, displeased, got short with Marjorie Swann and declared her to be a bad mother. Marj's rejoinder was that if she didn't do her part to stop the H-bomb, her children and "millions of other children all over the world" were going to die if "there is another war — a nuclear, global war." She was sentenced to six months in prison at Alderson, West Virginia. That much of the story is well-known history thanks to an article, sensitively written by the husband and wife team of Jhan and June Robbins, that was published in *Redbook* magazine.[51]

Although acts of civil disobedience like Bob's and Marj's are rooted in individual conscience and strengthened by the individual's gut sense that not acting against a perceived wrong would be intolerable, they are also as Gandhi knew, political tactics to develop a wider, more general opposition to the particular iniquity. Nonviolent direct actions are far more serious than publicity stunts, but their purpose includes drawing public attention to an issue. Marj's arrest and imprisonment did that in spades. Meanwhile, back at the household, round-the clock babysitting had to be organized, and councils of friends met to help Bob and the children grapple with Marj's long absence. "Nita" Nelson had not had children of her own, but she found herself toilet-training Scottie Swann. From the prison cell to the potty chair, the Peacemakers' base communities were nothing if not comprehensive in their mutual aid.

Bob wrote letters faithfully to Marj while she was in prison, and these letters survive. Dhyana Swann provided me with copies. Like Bob's letters from prison to his brother Jim, this correspondence fleshes in the daily experience of life in the peace movement.

In them, Bob addressed Marj as "Darling." He dutifully reported on various activities — a successful Peace Fair at which Pete Seeger sang, a training session that went off well — and on the children's conditions — how teenaged Barbara and pre-teen Judy were, over time, settling in to some responsibility for household chores, how Carol was moved from a public to a private school to ease her emotional problems and how rapidly Scottie's ability to speak was developing.[52]

As the subsequent decades have worn on and as narcissism and greed have become *de rigueur*, private lives have become atomized and self-centered; more public lives have become vulgar spectacles and simplified ballyhoo. Social action is now specialized and professionalized; civic life has been degraded to mere participation in the plebiscite — if that — and community has become a word sapped of vital meaning. But the Swanns, their Peacemaker friends and CNVA colleagues, because of their attention to more than personal concerns and their Gandhian thoroughness in striving to be the change they wished to see in the world, lived a positive liberation from convention.

It made for an unconventional and sometimes trying family life. Effective as Bob and Marj were as partners, their marriage was in the opinion of all their children troubled throughout. Bob and Marj both and each kept their causes and good works paramount.

As Dhyana Swann put it, "A lot of the focus was on activism as opposed to familyism."[53]

On a trip to Northern California in 2004, I was able to meet and interview all four of the Swann children as well as Marj Swann, long since remarried to John Edwin, an educator and senior bishop of the African Methodist denomination.[54] Each of the children spoke of Bob with love and admiration. Each seemed to me to be an interesting, individuated person and remarkably intelligent. If their movement childhoods had scarred them, it didn't show, for they shared their various recollections without expressing regret or resentment.

The eldest daughter Dhyana was at the time we spoke a counselor at Cabrillo Community College in Santa Cruz. She had arrived at a settled existence after years of traveling the world as a spiritual seeker — being "Zorba the Buddha," she said. Gracious and mellow, I found her, and guess she did a lot of work to wind up that way. As a teenage daughter of radical pacifists during the McCarthy era, she said she'd been mortified by the front-page headlines when her mother went to jail. "When we were quite young," she remembered, "there was always some march," and these sometimes met with hostility, including "people throwing stuff at us." Dhyana said she did a lot of "acting out."

Living in the gift economy that partly supported the Swanns' activism meant that scholarships to alternative schools were made available to the Swann kids. Dhyana went to a boarding school when she was 15, married a young radical pacifist at 17, divorced at 21 and then was involved in proletarian organizing and Marxist study groups in Detroit. "I was an activist," she said, "but it wasn't going to be nonviolent," which led to some heavy discussions with her father.[55]

Judy, the second child, wound up as a successful mortgage broker. We met at her home in Novato, California. The irony that the daughter of a man who had created the community land trust as an alternative to what he regarded as the moral dubiousness of treating land as property would make a career out of helping people obtain real property wasn't lost on her. A lot of her memories had to do with the Swann family's nomadism. They didn't keep the same address for very long.

"I always remember moving (and moving) and Dad always having to fix up the 'new' house we moved into." Judy calculated that she had been in thirteen schools by the time she was in twelfth grade. She, too, remembered spending "a lot of time picketing" and also collating mailings. Her mother's going to jail, she said, "was the first big political event that all of us had to deal with." The children took it hard that they were not going to have their mother for six months.

A few years after the big political event, Judy would also go away to school where she would meet Peter Pezzati, now her husband. During the early 1960s she and Peter attended a biracial camp in North Carolina in which the situation became dangerous enough that the campers, after two weeks, were given a police escort partway home. Like Dhyana, Judy initially carried on the family radicalism. She studied theater at Howard University, then moved to New York City. She worked and traveled with the avant-garde Living Theater and did organizing on the Lower East Side with Robert Collier, a Black Panther.[56]

The rough and ready circumstances of growing up in an activist household seasoned the Swann children for some adventurous living. Because Bob and Marj were part of a community of radical pacifists, there were other couples, like Juanita and Wally Nelson, to foster one or another of the young Swanns in timely ways.

Carol, who describes herself as a "teacher, facilitator, performance artist, somatic therapist and activist" lives in Albany, California.[57] She was six when Marj went to jail. When that happened, Carol said she went door to door telling the neighbors that her "mommy went to prison to save your children from nuclear war."[58]

That's not what I was doing when I was her age, living in a lilywhite suburb in Phoenix, Arizona. Still I do, like most baby boomers, remember my own infant fear of nuclear war, prompted by duck and cover drills in my third and fourth grade classrooms. I remember assembling with other neighborhood kids on our front porch to pray for peace when prayer was an unknown activity in our Agnostopalian household.

The consensus of the Swann children seemed to be that their father, an idealist and intellectual, was never very present to them in a personal way, and that his interactions with them remained cerebral. As his son Scott put it, "He lived on a different plane."[59]

Carol dogged Bob's heels, persisting over the years in trying to elicit his feelings. "I was always going after him emotionally…and I think he needed that…and he let me do it," she said.[60]

Unlike Dhyana and Judy, whose formative years were spent in a suburb — albeit one unusual for being racially integrated — Carol and Scott got to spend years of their childhood living with Bob and Marj and 20 or so peaceniks in a commune, the Polaris Action Farm in Voluntown, Connecticut. The Swanns' years there are the subject of the next chapter.

Scott Swann's reminiscences during our interview foreshadow that story. Scott, divorced and father of a son, Skyler, lives in Novato, California. Like his father he earns his living as a builder and contractor. Like his father, he has an artistic bent — for photography, which he studied, but which didn't pay the bills.

Scott also had memories of demonstrations and leafleting at the Electric Boat works in Groton, Connecticut, where the Polaris Action project began to challenge the construction and deployment of submarines armed with nuclear "city killer" missiles. "We would purposefully wait for people to get off their shifts," Scott remembered, and that the majority of the workers, when confronted with the peace activists, "would engage in a civil disagreement." However civil some of the encounters between the sub builders and the pacifists, there were also altercations, threats and violence. These left Scott relatively unscathed. He remembered the farm at Voluntown as being "a great place for a kid."[61]

CHAPTER 6

Toward an Economics of Peace

Bob ARRIVED with his family at Voluntown having been a part-time peace activist and full time building contractor in Concord Park. He left, more than a decade later, as a practicing if uncredentialed economist. By then his search for peace, civil rights and community had evolved from protest to practical creation of small-scale economic institutions premised on trusteeship. The peace and justice work at Voluntown would, in good Gandhian fashion, lead to a considerable amount of work on community economic development by the Swanns and other colleagues.

One index of the Swanns' values is that for most of their years together, they lived in intentional community. The modern, secular forms of such communities were occasioned and necessitated by the industrial revolution. As capitalism revolutionized production and all the vernacular means that had accomplished it — the close-knit guilds, workshops and farms — some visionaries like Robert Owen proposed an equally revolutionary remedy for the massive social dislocation caused by enclosure and industrialization.

They envisioned and initiated intentional communities — groups living together not by accident of birth, marriage or geography, or as monastic orders — but by secular choice. Whether

intentional or traditional, extended families and communal households are the building blocks of sustainable communities, decision-
making gymnasia. The Polaris Action Farm led by the Swanns was
a Gandhian commune, what liberation theologians would later
call a base community.

Through the 1950s arming for nuclear war was still a fresh hor-
ror. Trying to forestall nuclear arms proliferation, indeed to ban
the bomb as well as to oppose the peacetime draft, were prime
objects of radical pacifist action. There was work to be done on
integration and racial justice as well. The national Committee for
Nonviolent Action (CNVA) emerged from an ad-hoc committee protesting A-bomb testing in Nevada, becoming a permanent
committee in 1958.[1] As seasoned activists and Peacemakers, the
Swanns were part of its genesis.

CNVA organized a series of focal projects, staged each summer: in 1957, attempted trespass at the Nevada nuclear testing site,
in 1958 the sailing of the *Golden Rule* into the nuclear bomb test
area in the South Pacific,[2] the Omaha Action where Marj became
a "Bad Mother" in 1959 and in the summer of 1960 the Polaris Action at New London, Connecticut.[3]

The Polaris Action Project began with Brad Lyttle, principal
organizer of the CNVA, who wrote

> I opened a copy of *Newsweek*, and there facing me, was an
> advertisement sponsored by the Navy for their new weapons
> system, "Polaris." Polaris consisted of nuclear submarines
> armed with nuclear missiles. Each sub carried 16 missiles,
> and each missile had a warhead of at least 200 kilotons.[4]

The Polaris submarine was a "city killer" without any defensive
significance, nor was there any defense against it. As the submarines were being constructed by Electric Boat's shipyard at Groton,
Connecticut Lyttle reasoned that location near the central New
England coast and proximity to Ivy League and other universities
where the rationale for strategic deterrence and the engineering

of weaponry were fomented made the area a likely location for a CNVA beachhead. So in 1960 the Committee for Nonviolent Action headed to New London, Connecticut, across the Thames River from Groton. Construction of nuclear submarines was, incidentally, a mainstay of the local economy there.

On June 1, 1960, Bob Swann and another CNVAer opened and equipped a small Polaris Action office in a storefront handy to Electric Boat.[5] CNVAers engaged in much group discussion as they planned their various actions, which ranged from leafleting at the Harvard-Yale crew races to publicizing voyages made to Groton by sympathetic, seafaring pacifists. They engaged in bold acts of civil disobedience at the launching of the subs. One time two young CNVAers, Bill Henry and Don Martin (who was later to marry Barbara Swann) managed to elude the cordon of Navy vessels guarding the *Ethan Allen* at its gala launch festivities by swimming to board the vessel. Martin hauled himself up the bow on the red, white and blue bunting that bedecked it. This Polaris action made the front page of the *New York Times*.[6]

In a radio interview Lyttle said

Again and again Polaris Actionists have returned good for evil, blessed those who cursed them, fearlessly pressed a nonviolent attack against cynical and demoniacal military policies. Polaris Action was not cast in a conventional religious mold, but it had depth just as George Fox's ministry had depth, the Gandhian movement and the Underground Railroad.

Perhaps the strongest testimony to Polaris Action's depth is that the project inspired Bob and Marj Swann to move to New London to carry it on. I believe that theirs was a great spiritual decision and act, the kind that is essential to a movement. With their four children, they left their home, friends, economic security and a friendly community for a strange, sometimes hostile city and economic uncertainty....

People who could make decisions like this once gave America moral leadership in the world; perhaps they will be able to again....[7]

Marj Swann put it less heroically, saying that at the end of the summer of 1960 "a group of us decided it wasn't a good idea to stir up the whole community and then just move away."[8]

What soon resulted from the summer of civil disobedience in Groton was the Polaris Action Farm in Voluntown, Connecticut, a widely known intentional community whose servant-leaders were Bob and Marj Swann. For a most eventful 12 years, with many comings and goings, members of the community would participate in the long hot summers of Civil Rights activism in the Deep South, the protests of the Vietnam war era and the emergence of the counterculture.

In 1962, the 57-acre Voluntown farm was purchased by Mary Meigs, an artist and author who was the partner of the noted pacifist writer Barbara Deming. Deming had become acquainted with the Swanns at a Peacemakers workshop they conducted in New London. Meigs, who with Deming would become longtime friends of the Swanns and quite involved in the development of the New England CNVA (NECNVA), paid $12,500 for the property and turned it over to the Swanns.[9]

In addition to being a base of operations for the Polaris Action project, and when the Vietnam war escalated increasingly a refuge for a new generation of draft resisters, the Polaris Action Farm was a gathering place where elders and strategists of the peace movement could meet, plan and teach visions of world peace brigades and self-help initiatives for impoverished communities in the US and abroad. The Farm was a nonviolence training center, a hotbed of direct actions — walks, fasts, vigils and demonstrations — and a venue for an unending round of conferences on subjects like draft counseling, ecology, communes, cooperatives and the myths and realities of prison life.[10]

While the Polaris Action Farm was anomalous in its neigh-borhood of blue collar and rural southeastern Connecticut com-munities, it was in keeping with the American mode of Gandhian ashrams. From the interwar years onward radical pacifists had es-tablished a number of these. As Paul Salstrom, an early NECNVA staffer, put it, "We young people who came to Polaris Action/New England CNVA were generally from urban or suburban back-grounds, but many of us came to appreciate the rural life there and also the role of rural centers in a Gandhian approach to social change and (in particular) to movement-building."[11]

In addition to being seasoned (and in Marj's case, recently cel-ebrated) direct actionists, the Swanns, as Gandhians, aimed for a degree of communal self-sufficiency. Hence from the outset of Polaris Action they wanted a farm *wing* or *branch*. Dorothy Day was also a Peacemaker and CNVA activist, and it is likely that the Catholic Worker movement's peasant anarchism figured in the development of the Polaris Action Farm's constructive pro-gram.[12]

In late June of 2004 I visited Voluntown just to get a feel for the place. The three-story farmhouse, built around 1750,[13] had been well tended in recent years. Its focal point was a huge stone fireplace and a roomy kitchen. Framed *Time* magazine covers featuring Gandhi and Vinoba Bhave were hung on the kitchen walls — appropriate household icons for this anti-establishment. "We have come to loot you with love" Vinoba is saying. Buckshot holes, mementos of the 1968 attack by a cadre of right-wing para-military Minutemen, still pock the farmhouse living room walls. There were several motley outbuildings as well as a conference center and family home that Bob had built.

I arrived just as the Equity Trust, an offshoot of the Swann-founded Institute for Community Economics, was in its last days in residence. The place was changing hands, but not its mission of social change. Its new stewards would be the Voluntown Peace Trust, and an intentional community attempting to live sustainably and hospitably, serving as a retreat and conference center "poised to strengthen movements across issues."[14]

The Conference Center, named after A. J. Muste, was a meeting facility that looked like a parish hall at the tail end of a rummage sale — table after table held accumulated files of 30 years, along with assorted back issues of rare movement magazines. The center's library was being dispersed, donated and forwarded as thoughtfully as possible by Ellie Stephanopoulos, the lone staffer of the Equity Trust. By sheer chance, I was able to find, in the sea of printed materials, some clippings and articles about the Swanns' years, including the famous "You are A Bad Mother" story about Marj's arrest, reprinted from *Redbook*.

I sat at a desk in the Muste Center and counted 40 shelves bowed under a weight of evidence that legions of brave minds had fixed themselves upon the ideal of justice, probed the causes and the conditions of war, proposed remedies and chronicled the hopeful plenitude of campaigns to build a just peace, ever arguing the case for change, proposing and analyzing strategies, limning a world fair and fine. On the floor sat a cardboard box of Gandhiana. There were collections of books by and about Dorothy Day and Bayard Rustin and a shelf devoted to Simone Weil.

My initial impetus in going to Voluntown was to see some of Bob Swann's buildings. The Muste Center, which was designed by Norbert Carichner,[15] was one. Like some of Bob's own creations, the ambition of its design was way ahead of the performance of its materials. I was told that the Muste Center's roof sagged as soon as it was raised, and that the radiant heating embedded in the floor never worked very well.

However, set well back from the other buildings on the farm is the snug yet airy Wrightian family home that Bob designed and with farm staff built using only $3,000 worth of materials. Bob meant the house to be an experiment in low cost housing. A Sunday supplement piece saw it "therefore as likely a symbol as any of the CNVA pacifists' ongoing effort to integrate the everyday concerns of life with their goal of creating nonviolent revolution in this country."[16] The house had been standing vacant and forlorn for a while.

Over the years of its prime, young people came to the Polaris Action Farm to find themselves, or to find at least a measure of respect for their need to question the established order. The Polaris Action Farm hosted the kind of work-study activity and extended discussion of underlying principles that strengthened the peace movement's spine. There people could clarify their convictions and learn how to requite violence with compassion, or at least to forbear from retaliation. Despite its pacific intentions, the community was a lightning rod. The neighbor across the road called the residents "shiftless, no-good scum." Their purpose, she told a reporter, was "to completely agitate society and let no one be happy with what he has."[17]

The dozen or more people who lived there as staff received $1 a week in spending money and subsisted in part on the vegetables they grew. They were doing their collective best to stop the nuclear submarines, the Vietnam War and Jim Crow and also to tend the garden, do KP and keep a half dozen donated cars in repair all the while being "jolted awake frequently by drunken teenagers who jeer[ed] and taunt[ed] them."[18] There had been a barn, but in 1966 arsonists burned it down.[19] The Minutemen attack, clumsily handled by the state police, had "made clear to the CNVA staff that their work was really dangerous."[20] Collateral damage from the attack, according to Scott Swann, was that it "ruined our family vacation," for the Swanns were away at the time.[21]

The Polaris Action Farm worked to help National CNVA coordinate and service various peace walks and voyages. Greenpeace's maritime interventions were prefigured by various antinuclear movement vessels that on several occasions sailed, or at least attempted to sail, into the line of fire in hopes of preventing bomb tests. These interventions on land and sea were offerings of civil disobedience. There were walks rather than marches, long pilgrimages like the Quebec to Guantanamo walk, whose participants would cover hundreds of miles bearing witness of their dissent in scores of communities. A lot of writing was necessary to craft the leaflets that peace walkers would distribute. There was logistical work to find hospitality for the walkers and effectively interpret the purpose of the walks for peace and disarmament to the media and the public. Today the NECNVA's approaches to influencing public opinion and launching constructive programs — simple, but not easy and done with almost no funding — seem antique, primitive and innocent, yet they helped to nudge the course of history.

For 40 years a few thousand readers in America got a weekly bulletin on such good works and the wisdom to guide them. The publication was *MANAS*, and although it ceased with its creator's death, its value is undiminished. Henry Geiger was the author and publisher, from 1948 to 1988, of that philosophical newsletter which now seems to have issued from another world entirely. In many senses, not the least technological, *MANAS* was another world. In its clean letterpress pages devoid of illustration, ads and any but the most austere ornaments or sidebars, readers met Bob Swann, E. F. Schumacher, John and Nancy Jack Todd, Kirkpatrick Sale, Peter Berg, Wes Jackson, Wendell Berry and Theodore Roszak, to name only a few of the company of contemporary thinkers whose importance Geiger recognized. Side by side with the living were Thoreau, Tolstoy and Gandhi, great exponents of this "tradition without a doctrine."

Geiger, a theosophist, had, as mentioned before, also been a CO in World War II. He was a self-taught man of letters. It was in a CPS camp in California that he began his anonymous newsletter-producing vocation with *Pacifica Views* which he and others edited, publishing "some of the most cogent pacifist writing during the war years."[22] Geiger's singular and prolific intellectual contributions, like Bob's, raise a point about COs, their camps and prisons and the free intelligentsia concentrated and housed there by the militaristic state.

It's the Thoreaus, those freethinking simple-living prophets who attract just enough support from the aunts and the Emersons to keep them from perishing in the free-thought business, who wind up in jail on principle. The Swanns and the Geigers manifest a roaming, unorthodox and decidedly unremunerative kind of genius, performing intellectual and philosophical services for humanity that humanity may but dimly appreciate, if not actively ignore.

Geiger was a great fan of the Swanns and frequently relayed NECNVA goings-on to *MANAS* readers, such as this 1961 think piece of Bob's which was reprinted from the *Polaris Action Newsletter*.

> ...[W]hile I advocate the strongest kind of negative action (civil disobedience, nonviolent obstruction, etc.) I also advocate the strongest kind of constructive action. What kind of constructive action? To me the clearest approach to our problems is in the suggestions of Lewis Mumford, Arthur Morgan, Jayaprakash Narayan and others who are working for regional community redevelopment and revitalization. [J.P. Narayan was a cosmopolitan leader of modern India, one of the men who, like Vinoba Bhave, would pick up Gandhi's work of attempting to spawn a rural resurgence in India. While the saintly Vinoba walked India soliciting for the *bhoodan*, or land gift movement, Narayan advanced the *gramdan*, or village gift movement whereby land was given to a village rather than to individual farmers who, when strapped for cash to purchase seed or tools, might lose the land to money lenders. Narayan had, as part of the movement to liberate India, engaged with various ideologies, including Marxism. He emerged as a convinced decentralist and Gandhian.[23]] In this, the concept of regionalism is central. This means the

economic, political, physical and social reorganization of our
communities, regions and the world itself along organic, human lines of thinking that will bring the machine and our
vast technology under the control of Man, instead of serving
some abstract purpose such as the "free enterprise system",
"the state", and "dictatorship of the proletariat."[24]

The Voluntown years were heady and strenuous, a time when Bob
began to give free rein to his concern with economics, even as he
and Marj coordinated NECNVA activities. One journalist, in a
story on the Farm, characterized Bob as having an "explosive vitality."[25] That and more would be a minimum requirement to sustain
the pace of activity, both public and intellectual, and the amount
of travel that he engaged in.

As early as 1961, Bob conceived of a Gandhian home industry
project to help displaced sharecroppers in the mid-South. Agricultural mechanization provided a pretext for evicting blacks who
were seen as stepping out of line on account of their attempts to
register to vote. CORE sent a NECNVA staffer, Eric Weinberger,
to launch a leathercrafting co-op that sold suede tote bags by mail.
The Haywood Handicrafters League was a worker-owned nonprofit corporation with a membership of 75 women. By 1962 the
business, which started with $20, had grossed $20,000 and was
paying its members $10–15 dollars a month.[26] This project gave
rise to others, notably the Poor People's Corporation based in
Jackson, Mississippi, which had nationwide Liberty House outlets
for its tote bags and other leather products.[27]

About the time the Swanns and other CNVAers settled at
the Farm in the spring of 1962, Bob was summoned to the San
Francisco area to oversee construction of a boat, the *Everyman*, in-
tended to sail into a nuclear test zone in the Pacific in a protest
similar to that of the *Golden Rule*. Although the *Everyman* and its
crew (which didn't include Bob) were interdicted by the authori-
ties just outside the Golden Gate, the project made good copy, and

the arrest of the seafaring nonviolent direct actionists was news that drew attention to the disarmament cause.

1962 also saw Bob traveling to England for a meeting of the World Peace Brigade Council. The Brigade, established at a conference in Beirut the year before, was spurred by pacifists Bayard Rustin, A.J. Muste, a British activist Michael Scott and Jayaprakash Narayan. Its aim was to establish a nonviolent striking force to "revolutionize the concept of revolution itself."[28] Gandhi had proposed the creation of a nonviolent army as early as 1948.[29]

Bob shared his enthusiasm for the idea in a letter to his friend and protégé, Paul Salstrom: "the World Peace Brigade is...perhaps the most important pioneering effort of the world peace movement... because it...could become a genuine 'world' effort. For the first time we are attempting to look at the

NECNVA

Bob at Point Judith Fishing Cooperative in Rhode Island discussing conversion of New England navy yards, 1964

world as a whole and see where we can apply nonviolence to... solve — or dissolve — injustice, tension, aggression, potential war-making.... [E]ach individual volunteer of the WPB...speaks, in an nonviolent action, with the moral authority of the whole human race."[30] This vision, alas, has yet to be fully realized.

1963 found Bob back in federal prison in Danbury Connecticut, serving a brief sentence for "aiding and abetting" civil disobedience, presumably at the Electric Boat works. Once again, incarceration allowed an intellectual growth spurt, "a major rethinking," he wrote to Salstrom, "of the strategy and action of the peace movement," and the production of "around 14–15 major memos."[31]

A book that influenced Bob at about this time was Jane Jacobs' *The Death and Life of Great American Cities*,[32] which evidently

helped frame Bob's and thus the CNVA's consideration of the
"specters of 'Urban Renewal' or 'Redevelopment,' which to most
Negroes have come to mean 'Negro Removal.'"[33] Following a
week's discussion on urban problems at a NECNVA Summer
Training Program in Nonviolence, prompted in part by local resistance movements to various "ill-planned urban renewal" projects
and "arbitrary expressways," Bob proposed "that nonviolent leadership in civil rights and peace join with concerned and qualified
planning professionals to help give direction, leadership and coor-
dination to the various groups now active in resisting injustices in
center city situations."[34]

The potential for nonviolent direct action combined with a
constructive program to catalyze social transformation was the
driving force in the whirlwind of the Swanns' NECNVA activities. In 1965 the organization "planned, encouraged, assisted and/
or supported" over 40 demonstrations throughout the region protesting the US military presence in Vietnam. It continued demonstrations at every Polaris sub launch at Electric Boat in Groton,
sent four people to civil rights demonstrations in Selma, Alabama
and offered several weekend work camps and seminars in nonviolence for high school and college students.[35]

Both Bob and Marj spoke widely about their work. In 1965,
one subject of Bob's talks was his experiences in Mississippi, where
he had gone to supervise interracial crews rebuilding burned out
churches.[36] Nearly 40 years later when we spoke Bob said "That
was the setting in which I began to feel that I ought to be doing
what Gandhi called constructive work."[37]

That constructive work would be in community economics.
This was about the time, according to Salstrom, that Bob read
Gorham Munson's 1945 book Aladdin's Lamp. The book, a lively
read, is an exposition of Social Credit, somewhat of a centrist
idea as monetary proposals go. What interested Bob was not so
much Social Credit as Munson's explanation and condemnation
of money creation by private central banks.[38] "The banking system

assumes that it owns the people's credit," wrote Munson[39] and he argued that to resolve the money question, the system must be changed.[40]

"We must distinguish sharply between banking, which is a technical operation," wrote Munson, "and financial policy, which has to do with linking the productive resources of a country and the needs of its people for money."[41] Such a distinction, and the ringing declaration that "money is a social instrument and morally belongs to the people.... it is redeemed every time it is accepted by the public for goods and services"[42] (here Munson quotes economist Arthur Kitson) were catalytic ideas. Munson questioned the economic wisdom of the professionals[43] and lodged hope for the future in "Monetary Radicalism."[44] Although Bob Swann's days as a practicing monetary radical lay several years in the future, he was beginning to incorporate alternative money proposals in his writing on social issues.

Bob was not alone in his observation that while the civil rights movement was winning black people the right to sit anywhere they wanted in the diner, too many of them still lacked the means to make enough money to buy a hamburger. Dispossession from the land — the primary means of production — affected country people worldwide. Seeing that big picture Bob began to grapple with the intertwined problems of rural credit and land reform.

The civil rights and social justice work that concerned radical pacifists generally begged many a potent question as to how best to promote development and relieve poverty. Strategies for bootstrap community development that did not depend on the uncertain benevolence of nation-states were of keen interest to Gandhians and decentralists.

Many years later in an interview with Shann Turnbull, Bob said "I came back from the South convinced that what was needed was an economic program that would make it possible for blacks to get capital and credit..."[45] Swann began to pursue these possibilities in a correspondence with Arthur Morgan's son Griscom

about alternatives to the patterns of land tenure and money movement dominant in the West.[46] Around the same time, Bob Luitweiler, a fellow draft refuser and friend of Bob Swann's from the
wartime days, returned from Tanzania, where he had spent years
in village development work and consideration of patterns of land
tenure. Luitweiler headed to Voluntown to sojourn at the Farm,
bringing tidings of Julius Nyrere's *ujamaa* African development
model[47] which stressed collectivized, village-based production.

Also at that time, Ralph Borsodi, a grand old man of decentralism, returned from several years in India. He, too, had been
grappling with development questions, specifically what he saw as
the pressing need for a rural renaissance. Borsodi arrived in the
US with an elaborate, visionary scheme to fund locally supervised
provision of agricultural credit to the many thousands of *gramdan*
villages that Gandhi's successors Vinoba Bhave and J. P. Narayan
had helped to catalyze.[48] Borsodi, then nearly 80,[49] was nonetheless also a man of explosive vitality, fierce in his convictions and
economic views. He and Narayan had together formulated the
new *gramdan* microfinance plan.

Since his time in Ashland Prison Swann had been aware of
Borsodi's work. Fellow "one hundred percenter" war resister Tim
LeFever had been Bob's docent to Borsodi's work. Sometime in
1965 or 1966, a mutual friend of Swann's and Borsodi's, the publisher F. Porter Sargent, also a World War II CO, arranged a
meeting of the two. In addition to carrying on the family business of publishing guides to private schools, F. Porter Sargent had
launched a new line of books, *Extending Horizons*, with the 1955
publication of Kropotkin's *Mutual Aid*.[50] Bob's face-to-face meeting with Ralph Borsodi was as timely and life-changing as Arthur
Morgan's correspondence course had been. As Bob said

> Borsodi was completely confident — he knew everything....
> he could answer all the questions which I had and explain
> them to me, so that was a major leap in my life.... [His]

acceptance of me as an equal co-worker gave me a confidence
that I'd never had before."[51]

Through his books, projects and writings in the journal *Free America*, Ralph Borsodi was well known to American decentralists and
regionalists of the mid-20th century. A social critic, homesteader
and prominent practicing spokesman for small family farming,[52]
Borsodi was by birth a New Yorker. His father had been a follower
of Henry George and an active promoter of subsistence homesteading.[53] As a second-generation Georgist, Ralph Borsodi's
antipathy to the outsized industrialism and galloping consumerism of the 20th century was enunciated in his most popular books
This Ugly Civilization[54] and *Flight from the City*.[55]

Little known in our time, Henry George (1839–1897) was one
of the most prominent social thinkers of his day. His runaway
bestseller *Progress and Poverty*[56] changed many lives, including
Tolstoy's, by challenging the legitimacy of rents and profits gained
through land speculation. George's precept, which Borsodi and
Swann in turn embraced, was that land itself is in the nature of
a gift, entrusted to humanity as a common heritage and that in-
creases in land value are created by society as a whole. Therefore to
discourage land hoarding and to recapture some of the increased
land value were for society's benefit. Henry George proposed that
there should be just a single massive tax on land that would ab-
sorb all rents.[57] Hence Georgists are also known as single taxers.
George's idea was that by taxing land rather than taxing improvements or wages, the bias against smaller scale productive and en-
trepreneurial uses of land would be eliminated, and so would unemployment and disparities in wealth.[58] Progress could then be
uncoupled from poverty.

Thus George's great themes — that while land might be possessed it should be treated socially as a trust — and that widespread
access to land for productive purposes was the foundation of an
equitable, responsible commonwealth — helped shape Borsodi's

and Swann's economic innovation. As we have seen, Borsodi's un-flagging interest in alternative forms of land tenure, rural credit and overarching economic ills like inflation had led him to India where he spent several years studying the "*gramdan*, or village land gift movement, which set aside millions of acres for the landless poor."[59]

Earlier still, in the 1930s with the Depression in full swing, Borsodi, who worked in Manhattan as an economic consultant, had started Bayard Lane and then Van Houten Fields, homestead communities near Suffern, New York. These were, writes David Shi, "based on leaseholds, with the legal title to the land vested in the community trustees. To help homesteaders with their capital needs, Borsodi formed…a nonprofit corporation that borrowed money…to purchase the acreage for the settlements…. Each homesteader was required to pay his share of the annual taxes, carrying charges, and amortization but was saved from any high initial capital outlay."[60] Other forms of cooperation, like buying clubs, carpools and bartering arrangements, along with work in their large gardens and at various other practices of rural self-sufficiency helped the homesteaders keep their cash outlays to a minimum. Within a matter of years, though, the leasehold approach lost its support in both communities, and by 1940 they decided to change to fee-simple ownership.[61]

Within months of their meeting, Bob Swann and Ralph Borsodi would formalize the International Independence Institute (III) to further the Borsodi-Narayan scheme for fostering a world-wide rural renaissance. It would be a Third Way of development, one not beholden to nation-state lending or largesse nor contingent on Maoist revolution or centripetal, urbanizing economies of scale.

Towards that end, in August of 1966 Bob organized a conference on *Plans for the International Independence Institute*, which was attended by, among others, Ralph Borsodi, Sugata Dasgupta of the Gandhian Institute of Studies in Benares, Faye Bennett and

Paul Salstrom. In the course of their discussions, the participants, following Borsodi and Dasgupta, crafted the structure of a system for providing and administering rural credit in thousands of villages in India and worldwide. Borsodi's scheme was to raise the funds internationally through a sale of debentures that could be launched, along with the III's program, in connection with an anticipated US tour by J. P. Narayan.[62] The details of the funding scheme are interesting but overtechnical for the purposes of this book. What is important is the III's focus on more democratic or community-governed land holding, on security of land tenure and on the judicious and non-usurious provision of agricultural credit — not subsidies or grants — but on what is now called microfinancing.

Unfortunately Narayan cancelled his US tour, prompted by the Indian government's threat to discontinue funding for his Sarva Seva Sangh village development program because of its Borsodian feature of issuing the loans not in rupees, but in a noninflationary (and thus competing) currency to be called the Constant. That put the kibosh on the III's vision for India. Undeterred "Swann lowered his sights and persevered. The American South had many of the same problems as an 'underdeveloped' country."[63]

Although these days we think of civil rights activism as having been focused mainly on achieving political and social equality — what some categorize as *process rights* — there was also considerable work going on in the American South to address the plight of landless blacks and the root causes of the economic inequality that kept African Americans powerless. The National Sharecroppers Fund, whose executive secretary was Faye Bennett, was among the organizations working on the problem and trying to lend a hand to southern black community organizers and leaders. Bennett is credited with organizing numerous agricultural cooperatives in the South. With Bob Swann and Slater King, Bennett would be key to the genesis of New Communities in Albany, Georgia, a 5,000-acre land trust organized to provide secure tenure and thus an economic base for black farmers in the region.

The International Independence Institute, which would be Bob Swann's institutional aegis for the next several years, looked to the South — to Albany, Georgia and its environs. There black community leaders and white allies would come together to establish New Communities, Inc., the first community land trust in the US. Bob would craft a novel form of land holding that answered the Georgist moral objection to outright individual possession, the understandable need of the trust's inhabitants for security of tenure, and the interest of the surrounding community in the uses of the land.

1966 was an eventful year for Bob at Voluntown. Not only was the International Independence Institute (whose development projects demanded intellectual and organizational energy from both Bob and Marj Swann) a reality, but the war in Vietnam was escalating and tempers in the nation — and region — were running high. NECNVAers continued their walks, fasts and vigils.[64] Arsonists burned the barn at the farm.[65] The Swanns and other Voluntown staff proceeded to build anew. The Muste Center was begun that year, and the Swann family home. Bob also constructed a home in Massachusetts at Woolman Hill Quaker Center for another notable CO, the author Milton Mayer.

While Bob became increasingly focused on economic problems, especially those having to do with land reform, Marj began to look beyond the NECNVA and the Voluntown farm for new arenas of peace action. An anecdote from the Swanns' latter days in Voluntown suggests the changes coming down on the farm: around 1970 Bob evidently was so caught up in the III's work that he failed to resist the little war tax that was levied via the telephone bills in those days. With good-humored pugnacity, Marj organized a demonstration, complete with sign-carrying Voluntown staff, and picketed Bob's office.[66]

CHAPTER 7

New Roots for Economics

I N 1951, VINOBA BHAVE, Gandhi's chosen successor, confronted violent communist-organized disturbances occurring
in Hyderabad, India simply by asking a local landowner to share
his property. The landowner donated 100 acres to the landless.
Thus was born the *bhoodan,* or land-gift program, the beginnings
of a consensual approach to land reform: redistribution without
revolution.[1]

In highly urbanized, industrialized North America, access to
arable land is not so clearly understood as being fundamental to
household and community subsistence and social order as it is in
peasant countries. This misconception may change, however, as
economic decline and the end of cheap oil mandate the relocalization of food production and of much else besides. Whereupon the
overdeveloped world may have to face its own land distribution
crisis.

In his prophetic book *Jerusalem* William Blake declared that
"He who would do good to another, must do it in Minute Particulars...For Art & Science cannot exist but in minutely organized Particulars." To institute a more just economics, Bob Swann,
Ralph Borsodi and other decentralists saw, required minute attention to structure and solid respect for the soil-spawned particulars

that provide subsistence and the raw material of trade. Land is the alpha and the omega of our shared existence.

When Bob Swann was in the southern US in the mid-1960s, he was among the civil rights activists who saw tens of thousands of black people who were not only landless but whose land-based labor in cotton and other agriculture was being eliminated, not least by federal subsidies that promoted agricultural industrialization. In early 1966, some dozens of the thousands of black families who had been evicted from plantations in the Mississippi Delta briefly occupied a vacant Air Force Base near Greenville and drew attention to this internal refugee problem. They were forcibly evicted.

Bob commented that "This situation symbolizes.... the morally bankrupt condition of a government which is willing to spend billions of dollars to hold back revolution in [Vietnam]...but cannot even let its own citizens use its military facilities."[2] Uncle Sam, unlike that landowner in Hyderabad who gave the 100 acres, would not make a donation to these landless folk.

To confront this plight Bob was involved with a group of ministers working on civil rights issues, the Delta Ministry, trying to develop a self-help truck farming project near Greenville, Mississippi. Four hundred acres of land had been purchased, but the funds to build homes for the scores of families to live and work there were hard to find. The US Office of Economic Opportunity (OEO) wouldn't help because the land wasn't to be owned individually. To contend with the challenge of finding investors, Bob and his colleagues started the Freedom Development Fund. *MANAS* wrote, "The vision which engages Bob Swann's hopes and energies is the prospect of a civil rights movement which gradually becomes a community-based economic movement able to attract the financial support of northerners along with moral and legislative backing."[3]

Bob Swann was working on the ground in the deep South and in the realm of ideas through his writings. "[O]nly an economic programme can reach to the heart of the world peace problem," wrote Bob in a 1967 paper "The Economics of Peace," which appeared in both *The Catholic Worker* and *Peace News*.[4] Bob's was a grand vision for an international fund that would allow people to invest in "the small farmer, the rural cooperative, the village industry, the small businessman...who constitute the backbone of any successful 'self-help' programme to eliminate poverty and injustice."[5] The program he proposed would involve carefully administered lending, supervised in the field, providing credit at reasonable rates. It would globalize the *bhoodan* movement, helping to take land out of speculation. It would offer alternative investment possibilities, "prepare the ground for a significant boycott of the present financial structure," and thus offer a "just" form of savings. It would launch a transformation towards a universal currency of stable commodity value because, Swann wrote, "At present, virtually all national currencies are in a continuous process of inflation caused by the internal necessities of a money system based on debt creation."[6]

Since the fund would be a nonprofit corporation operating within the worldwide commodity market, it could grow large enough to combat monopolies and cartels as well as lowering the cost of credit in the developing world. Eventually it would revolutionize banking and help right "the balance between rural development and urban development.... The present monopolistic land and money system acts as a magnet to attract resources into urban centers at the expense of rural areas," leading to slums and ghettoization.[7]

With his interest in Gandhi and his followers and in the landlessness that was hobbling African-Americans in the southern US, Bob was perforce interested in development. Former colonies and new nations in what was then called the Third World as well as the "Third World" that lay within the First World aspired to improve their living standards. Swann, through the International Independence Institute, was working on Borsodi's complex nongovernmental development scheme to provide Indian villages with microfinancing for small-scale agricultural production. The precept in that work, and in his "Economics of Peace," was that monetary instruments of exchange and the provision of credit for productive purposes locally and globally could and should happen without entrapping communities in debt or undermining them through inflation. Nor should monetary instruments be national, or deployed in the interest of nation-states.

"The Economics of Peace" contains most of the economic elements—land reform, monetary reform, small-scale productive credit, socially responsible investing and banking reform—that Bob would work on for the rest of his life. Throughout the 1960s and 1970s, the world was his purview (as the International Independence Institute's name implies). But like his new mentor Borsodi, Bob would work on projects that brought the vision—or some aspect of it—down to the minute particulars, in real places and with real colleagues and communities, like the people he worked with in Albany, Georgia.

This was the case with the community land trust mechanism, which began to evolve in Bob's mind during this period. Building that family home at Voluntown was a particular that focused his attention. The land at Voluntown was held by a simple nonprofit trust. But who should possess the equity in those improvements on the land, like houses, that were created by individuals with their funds and their labor? Borsodi's 1930s homestead projects had provided for individual ownership of such property with the land itself being leased from the homestead project that held it. In his autobiography Bob wrote that "there was one thing missing in this model: a lack of broad participation by the town or community."[8]

By 1968, Bob, Slater King, a black community leader from Albany, Georgia, and Erick Hansch were collaborating. Hansch was Swiss, a polymath retired electrician who had come to work at the III with Swann because Swann's ideas comported with his anthroposophical thinking on economics. September 1968 found them presenting a paper on the design of a land trust and rural agricultural development project to the Center for the Study of Democratic Institutions in Santa Barbara, California.[9]

Meanwhile, the group endeavor to realize what became the New Communities project included Slater King, Faye Bennett, executive secretary of the National Sharecroppers Fund, and Charles Sherrod, director of the Southwest Georgia Project. They, Andrew Young and several other black civil rights activists, all of whom saw the problem of access to land as primary, traveled to Israel to study the Jewish National Fund's land acquisition and settlement mechanisms firsthand.[10]

The saga of the genesis of New Communities is recounted in some detail in the III's book, *The Community Land Trust*, published in 1972.[11] It's a case study in social and practical complexity. A predominantly black group was putting together a big (4,800 acre, $1,080,000) real estate deal in a hostile environment while organizing the governance of the land trust in ways that answered the prospective occupants' needs for a combination of individual and cooperative farm plots and commitments of labor. Meanwhile the leaders, Bob among them, were hustling all over the country to put together the financing to acquire the land.

The scramble for money to acquire the land for New Communities led far and wide, even to Washington, DC, where the possibility of OEO grants or loans sufficient to accomplish the land purchase glimmered. The condition for obtaining the money was the submission of a comprehensive business plan for the farm with its cooperative, individual, retail, wholesale and value-added elements. A hefty $100,000 planning grant was received. Among the enduring outcomes of the planning process was Bob's friendship with a consultant, John McClaughry, a crusty libertarian Vermonter who would become a decentralist intellectual buddy and loyal supporter of Bob's work through all the years to come.

The business plan was extensive and complex — it had to be to delineate the means of livelihood for the hundreds of black farm families whom the founders of New Communities envisioned settling on the nearly 5,000 acres. Low cost housing cooperatives, schools and training facilities, individual shops, an industrial park and a cultural center were included. Nineteen sixty-nine, the year in which most of the work on organizing New Communities was accomplished, found Bob and the project's leaders meeting frequently for long discussions of the leasehold principle underlying the whole endeavor. The authors of *The Community Land Trust* wrote

> Convincing some of the more militant blacks that the leasehold system was not antithetical to black control and ownership and that such a system could — and indeed would — provide land tenure security presented a problem. The concept of land ownership and private property was and is strong (even though ownership is usually only nominal, with land often mortgaged by poor farmers and then lost to creditors). Although history has shown that the leasehold principle is needed to keep people from losing their land; to prevent land speculation, absentee ownership, and exploitation; and to assure land utilization for maximum usage, people would need time to learn to accept this form of land tenure.[12]

In devising his alternative to the individual possession of land which allows the right of sale of improvements and heritablility of lease, Bob's great contribution was to to figure out ways to structure community responsibility and participation into the agreement under which the land was held. He created a system of checks and balances. The community land trust board would not consist only of elected representatives of the land's occupants, whose self-interest might default to decisions that would fail to serve the greater good of land and locale. One third of its membership would consist of other interested parties from the community at large, and another third of its membership would be individuals with relevant expertise in accounting, law, real estate or planning.

Community land trusts (CLTs) are designed so that they do not require their occupants to be saints, ascetically forgoing tenure or possession of improvements. The leap that CLTs do require is open and active participation in the formulation and administration of the trust's land use plan and subsequent participation at periodic meetings. They represent a kind of contemporary re-creation of the village council.

The story of organizing and launching New Communities, Inc. was a high point of Bob's life. The group work, the intellectual creativity, the wide-ranging effort to procure the money first to option the land and then obtain the mortgages, the constant rallying of support for the project — it was all meat and drink to him. The land deal closed in January of 1970 with a flurry of interstate travel to ferry checks drawn in New York to Albany, Georgia in order to meet a deadline with increasingly reluctant sellers and the various attorneys involved.[13]

The head fairly swims from poring over some of the records of what Bob and his colleagues, with Marj providing the backup writing, editing and administrative skills, were attempting in those days. In a 1970 report to friends of the International Independence Institute, Bob described the farming underway at New Communities as well as outlining the federally funded joint planning process. From seeking the large sums needed for development of New Communities' physical plant to recruiting a "northern brigade" of young volunteers to harvest the 200-acre watermelon plot — in mid-July, in southwest Georgia — Swann was busy.[14]

Because the federal funding was spiked, New Communities began burdened with a land debt that finally proved to be unpayable through the complex mechanisms of land development utilizing the leasehold principle that Bob had designed. Still, in its heyday, New Communities was the largest black-owned single tract farm in the United States. By 1978 it included over 5,735 acres and was producing table vegetables, soybeans, grapes, corn, watermelons, pecans, peanuts, pork and beef. Sixteen families were gaining an income from the farm, and a uniquely American approach to land reform had been launched.[15]

In a matter of years the project came apart and the land was sold off. Years later when Bob recounted the story to the Canadian decentralist scholar Mary Beth Raddon, he spoke of the various "heartbreaking" turns of events that bedeviled New Communities.[16] Entanglement with the federal government had meant an enticement to dream big. It meant that the dream and all its details would be mortally vulnerable to political whims, as had been the case with Arthur Morgan's planned communities in the TVA and Ralph Borsodi's New Deal era homestead project in Ohio.

In the early 1970s Borsodi's International Foundation for Independence (of which the III was technically the educational arm) advanced credit to a program in Mexico. The program launched a successful, supervised agricultural microlending project that provided carefully selected small groups of farmers with credit for fertilizer for corn crops as well as for some livestock purchases. Just a few score farmers were involved. The focus was resolutely local and agrarian, experimenting, as Bob would put it, "with the application of such potent concepts as decentralized, small-scale credit and technology.... act[ing] as catalysts joining with other non-profit, voluntary agencies."[17]

By 1971 the Swanns and the III headquarters had left the Voluntown farm and moved to Ashby, Massachusetts. Various III members and staff were writing (Erick Hansch's papers on community credit and banking, and on land); organizing (Don Newey's and Roger Wilk's work organizing buying clubs directly linking organic farmers and urban consumers in Boston, New York, Washington and Detroit) and were serving as pundits on planning and economic development at various conferences.[18]

In addition to their concern with land reform and rural development Swann and Borsodi both believed that a stable system of non-national currencies would be crucial for the future. Monetary theory is a large and elusive subject. An explanation is beyond the scope of this book (and my limited economic fluency). It was handily within Swann's grasp and had been on his mind at least since his encounter with Munson's *Aladdin's Lamp*. For our purposes it helps to understand that in the US, our everyday money is *fiat* currency, essentially lent into existence, at interest, by commercial banks at the pleasure of the quasi-public Federal Reserve system. Its value is, in a sense, a matter of opinion, for its issue isn't constrained by any requirement that it be redeemable in something tangible like precious metal as US currency was at one time. Governments can finance their mischief — like war making — by increasing the money supply through the sale of treasury bonds rather than resorting to the unpopular measure of taxation. The tendency of these unmoored national currencies is inflation — a loss in purchasing power and in the value of savings. When the nation whose central banks run the money supply loses its creditability, its currency may become worthless.

There's far more real economic activity in the world than can be transacted even in gold or silver-backed money. Besides which gold, as a commodity, is subject to price fluctuations. One of the money-backing ideas that Swann and Borsodi espoused was the use of a *basket of commodities* commonly traded worldwide. The concept had first been raised in the 1930s by the economist Irving Fisher. The idea was that on average, the overall value of the two dozen or so basic commodities would be stable. Borsodi's innovation, which circumvented the problem of warehousing all that jute, nickel and copra, all those hides and mountains of rice and corn, was to arbitrage contracts for those commodities. The material backing for the currency (provisionally called the Constant) would thus exist in the world of commodities. Acquisition and arbitrage of commodities would not only tether the Constant's value to real production but could, if the system grew enough, exert a tempering effect on the trade in commodities.

Borsodi, through his organization Independent Arbitrage International, was preparing to get the show on the road and issue

Constants experimentally in Exeter, New Hampshire where he lived. But Bob did not confine his hopes for the creation of such a currency to the Constant's success. He imagined and wrote about the possibility of a new, Third World world bank that would issue a commodity-indexed currency. Swann's zeal was patent. He declared

> Money is a weapon of the state, used both to keep its own citizens under control and to maintain its control over other parts of the world...To take the power of creating money away from the nation-state might, therefore, be the most effective way of stopping its power to wage war—hot or cold.... [But] since politicians are not going to give up their most potent source of power.... doing it indirectly [is advisable]...by first creating a world currency, or non-national currency, which because of its stability...would eventually push national currencies out of the way.[19]

In the same paper Bob went on to propose a world bank using a raw materials commodity reserve system as the basis for a stable world currency.

> ...[T]he people of the third world would be gaining tremendous advantages.... since each country could use its commodity reserves as the basis for new money creation at the world bank, it would be able to expand its credit creation many times—without inflation.[20]

These must have been mighty times for an impecunious carpenter. Not only was Bob doing good work with sharecroppers in the deep South, he was, as a result of his writings on monetary reform, given an audience with one of the world's top bankers—and thanks to other prescient work on petrodollars, was sought out by a Saudi royal interested in discussing Swann's ideas. David was lunching with Goliath.

Swann was not only a gifted lay economist, but he was also a renowned peace activist, part of a diverse international movement against war and the inequities underlying so much conflict. When he traveled, which in those days was almost constantly, he had a feast of interesting encounters. In the early 1970s, Bob Swann was adept enough in monetary theory and enthusiastic enough about the promise of a stable world currency that he found an opportunity to tout it to the chairman of Barclays Bank in London.

In the spring of 1972 Swann's friend Sam Adams, a Citicorp banker turned farmer traveled with Bob to England. Adams recalled the trip.

> It was a period when hyperinflation and economic collapse — especially in England and Europe — appeared to be a distinct possibility.
>
> The times seemed ripe to advance the wisdom of an alternative currency....
>
> While in England, we met with a diversity of economic actors — from...Fritz [E.F.] Schumacher to the Chairman of Barclays Bank — to discuss the theory and implementation of "the Constant."
>
> The Chairman of Barclays...was sufficiently interested to invite the two of us...for a private lunch at the Bank's world headquarters.... Here...[were a] carpenter and a small farmer from rural New England suggesting to one of the loftiest representatives of capitalism the need for a new currency that would have egalitarian implications for the world.
>
> ...[T]he banker agreed that the idea of "the Constant" had merit but he had his doubts that without a worldwide financial collapse or a spiritual transformation — or both — it would ever fly in his lifetime.[21]

In addition to meeting a top banker and E. F. Schumacher whose classic book of economic essays, *Small is Beautiful: Economics as if*

People Mattered,[22] was imminent, Adams said he and Bob met as well with peace activists from Northern Ireland and Lady Eve Balfour, the great patron of the British Soil Association. This dance card is indicative of Swann's range of concern, from the plain fact of soil to the *mysterium* of monetary policy and always the search for peace.

By this time Swann was involved in a myriad of initiatives to change the nature of economics, aspect by aspect. With the publication in 1972 of *The Community Land Trust: A Guide to a New Model for Land Tenure in America* co-authored by Swann, Shimon Gottschalk, Erick Hansch and Edward Webster, a nascent movement was given its handbook. Swann's travels would include mentorship of groups hoping to establish community land trusts and so move beyond just common ownership to ownership for the common good.

In a paper delivered at the historic First National Conference on Land Reform held in San Francisco in 1973, Swann distilled the basic features of the community land trust. He described the CLT as "a quasi-public body, chartered to hold land in stewardship for all mankind present and future while protecting the legitimate use-rights of its residents. The word 'trust' is used more to connote the idea of trusteeship or stewardship than to define the legal form. Most often the land trust will be a non-profit corporation rather than a legal trust."

Four features differentiate the community land trust from real estate or conservation trusts, Bob explained: the trust holds land only, not improvements; the land user is protected by a 99-year, renewable lease; the trust's charter protects the land itself and the trustees ensure that the land trust's charter and provisions of the lease contracts are fulfilled.[23]

Hashing out a community land trust's charter, as with the genesis of New Communities, Inc., is a democratic process. Enough groups around the country were able to acquire land and do the organizational work that by 1975, Paul Salstrom, by then the editor of the magazine *Green Revolution*, reported that "the III files show over 50 community land trusts formed, and the actual number is estimated as at least twice as many." [24]

Bob Swann was always a decentralist, even paradoxically when he envisioned international systems. These took the form of private, nonprofit, voluntary organizations, and their functions — that of a stable currency, for instance — were indispensable, for a world without some trade among regions and communities would be inconceivable. The question was how to facilitate such essentials and empower regions and localities; how to articulate various levels of economic activity such that local production for local needs was kept primary and protected by structures like the community land trust.

Swann was not alone in engaging the challenges of economic reform as creatively as he did, but he, more than many, translated his ideas into grass-roots action. With the appearance in 1973 of Schumacher's book *Small Is Beautiful*, a new mode of economic discourse arrived with a moral philosophy to frame the kind of work Bob Swann had been doing for the previous several years.

E. F. Schumacher was a second-generation economist who worked as an expert in economics for much of his life, developing a specialty in energy. At the pinnacle of his career, Schumacher turned to eastern philosophy. Before long he began writing on the moral and practical failures of orthodox and macro economics. When *Small is Beautiful* appeared it gave a new generation permission, even encouragement, to question the dicta of an economic worldview premised on selfishness and endless growth and to advocate for an economics "as if people mattered."

The book consisted of 19 lectures, talks, speeches, essays and articles that Schumacher had produced over the previous decade on a range of big subjects such as production, resources, technology, development and organization. All the writing is undergirded by Schumacher's considerable expertise. A few of the pieces are technically detailed but never tiresome. What gave the book its value and influence was Schumacher's light sure touch in calling conventional economic thinking to account in ethical terms. Availing himself of perennial wisdom, Schumacher invoked Christian tradition, the *I Ching*, Buddhist precepts and Gandhi's truths in his writings towards an economics — and techniques — that would foster the dignity and virtue of human beings and would acknowledge certain ineluctable realities like the finite nature of planet Earth's sources and sinks. Schumacher grasped both the physical and moral implications of ecology. This was one of the main reasons that *Small Is Beautiful* was so valuable at its moment and looks so prescient in ours.

Bob Swann had become acquainted with Schumacher in the 1960s through Schumacher's writings in England's *Resurgence* and also *Peace News*. The two first met in 1967. When *Small is Beautiful* appeared, Bob championed the book, and with the help of futurist-economist Hazel Henderson, organized a US speaking tour for Schumacher that included visits with many decision makers, among them California's then-governor Jerry Brown. The tour boosted the book's fortunes considerably.

Bob Swann's fellow Peacemaker Dorothy Day wrote appreciatively of his work, along with Borsodi's and Schumacher's, for having helped her understand the necessity of contending with economics-as-usual. In the 1930s Peter Maurin, the agrarian anarchist co-founder with Day of the Catholic Worker movement, she wrote, had gone to Wall Street to talk with editorial writers and investors "about economics and money lending at interest.... None of us really grasped what Peter Maurin and his friend Ralph Borsodi were talking about at that time." But in a meditation published in September 1974, said Day, "Talking to Bob has begun to help me see the light on economics." The young people who come as volunteers to the Catholic Worker houses needed, she thought, "to major in the New Economics of a Ralph Borsodi, a Schumacher and Bob Swann."[25]

Like Schumacher and Borsodi, Bob Swann had the gift of an

ability to illuminate economics, which, as he once dryly remarked, "is not necessarily an easy subject." Bob could imagine and work through in detail economic practices that would, according to Maurin's simple edict, "Make the kind of society where it is easier to be good."[26]

To that end, Bob and his colleagues at the International Independence Institute functioned somewhat as a think tank, doing the intellectually demanding work of proposing as well as enacting economic reform. Bob's extant and as-yet-uncollected writings from the latter half of the 1970s delved into monetary issue ("Energy, PetroCurrency and the World's Future;"[27] "A World Currency Based on Community Land Trust Resources;"[28] and "Proposal for a Village Monetary System Based on Trusteeship,"[29]) land reform ("Community Land Trust: A New Ownership Approach?"[30] "Land Trusts as a Part of a Threefold Strategy for Regional Integration"[31] and "Appropriate Technology and New Approaches to Ownership"[32]), and microfinance ("Rural Credit as a Key to Development: A Report on a Mexican Experiment"[33]). In addition to their visionary import, together these heresies provided readers and those who heard them delivered at various conferences, with a functional education in banking, credit, currency issue and land tenure. If *Small Is Beautiful*, with its wisdom and charm, is a work that did much to establish a good and sensible climate of opinion, it is about economics rather than being an economics. Bob Swann's as-yet uncollected writings on economics, by contrast, are a sort of *Popular Mechanics* — or *Popular Economics*. Many of these papers have been published online by the E. F. Schumacher Society.

In November of 1975 his article on energy and petrocurrency earned Bob an invitation from a highly influential personage, the Saudi prince Mohamad Al-Faisal, to discuss the establishment of a stable monetary system.[34] There's no concrete evidence that anything came of this meeting. But for one's thought to be taken seriously by Saudi potentates and candidates for canonization (which

Dorothy Day now is) as well as numerous others in between does attest its consequence.

Around this time Bob and his colleagues — among them a lively character named Terry Mollner — conjured a different organization, the Institute for Community Economics, which evolved out of the International Independence Institute. The Swanns and therefore ICE moved from rural Ashby, Massachusetts to Cambridge.

Promotion of the community land trust movement was the focus of much of the ICE's activity and invention. In addition to providing technical assistance on the formation of CLTs, the ICE confronted the need for money to be available to make land purchases when local groups were organized and ready to proceed with their CLTs. Members of the ICE convened a think tank to develop ideas about funding such purchases and other community investments. The group brainstormed *social screens* — positive criteria for channeling funds from socially conscious investors into pro-active endeavors. This germ of an idea would blossom some years later into the Calvert Social Investment Fund, making Bob, in Terry Mollner's words, "one of the fathers of socially responsible investing."[35]

In 1977 something happened that would usher in a dramatic change to Bob's life. A young woman, Susan Witt, was so captivated by what she had heard of Bob's thinking about E. F. Schumacher and his concept of intermediate technology in a radio interview that she volunteered to work at the ICE. "I was immediately impressed with her ability," Bob recalled. "She catches on to things faster than anyone.... My ideas and interests...connected with hers very quickly...we could see right away that we were on the same wavelength."[36]

Witt had met Swann once before, in 1967 when he and Ralph Borsodi were traveling around New England raising money for the III. At that time the 21-year old Witt, deeply engaged in her studies of philosophy and literature, had yet to develop an interest in economic reform. Even so, Witt and Swann had been linked through their mutual friend Erick Hansch who, like Witt, was an anthroposophist, a follower of Rudolf Steiner's thought. The erudite Hansch would occasionally take a break from the economic endeavors of the ICE to visit with Susan and her husband in New Hampshire where he could talk with them about literature and anthroposophy.[37]

By 1977 Witt, who had been teaching literature at a Waldorf School in New Hampshire, had developed an interest in economics. What's more, thanks to a small inheritance, she had "decided to spend the next two years writing about those working to change the economic system to incorporate social and ecological principles.... [She] wanted to record the effort to bring about positive transformation."[38] Free to work and learn in a realm that she'd come to see as determining, Witt made her fateful call and offered to do clerical work at the ICE, inaugurating dramatic change in her life as well.

It was in the following year, 1978, that the ICE founded the Community Investment Fund, with Witt as its staff person. In addition to investing in CLTs, the fund aimed also to invest in worker-owned businesses, cooperatives and other socially responsible projects.[39]

Later the Community Investment Fund, a revolving loan fund, would take on a life of its own under the leadership of Chuck Matthei, a charismatic protégé of Bob's. Matthei steered the ICE and the fund towards urban community land trusts as a strategy for keeping housing affordable and thus addressing poverty. Over the years since it began the ICE's revolving loan fund has placed more than 370 loans totaling more than $35 million.[40] These days community land trusts are proving their resilience for their residents and are, thanks to the CLT structure, far less vulnerable to foreclosure than conventional mortgage holders.[41]

Because Bob had by the late 1970s developed such wide expertise in decentralist economics, the ICE office became something of a mecca for people who wanted to "just sit down with him and talk about community or land or money," Susan recalled in an interview. Since they were busy in the office starting the community investment fund, Susan recommended that Bob offer an evening course on land, money, community and worker ownership to satisfy that need for serious discussion.[42] Advance readings for the course included works by Henry George and Ralph Borsodi, Peter Barnes' *Who Owns the Land?* and Daniel Zwerdling's *Workplace Democracy*.[43] Susan brought her pedagogical skills to shaping a course in which Bob could expound the ideas and principles of what the ICE was working on day to day.

It wasn't long before Swann and Witt went from being colleagues to becoming lovers. "I can't distinguish between whether it was an emotional or intellectual connection," said Bob, "but I fell in love with her, there's no doubt about that. And so we became coworkers, partners and have been ever since."[44] The Swanns' marriage finally collapsed, nearly taking Marj down with it. She was extremely distressed and aired her grievance widely in the New England peace community where she had continued, through her work at the American Friends Service Committee, to play a prominent role. Although the dissolution of the Swann's marriage may have been for the best, even 20 years later when I began working on Bob Swann's story and talking informally with folks who had known the Swanns, memories of that upheaval hadn't entirely faded.

CHAPTER 8

Threshold in the Berkshires

IN 1980 SWANN AND WITT were living in a fourth floor walkup
in Cambridge, Massachusetts[1] carrying on the work of the
Institute for Community Economics. Susan worked in a book-
binding factory in Boston to support the endeavor.[2] Then a provi-
dential request came from a family near Great Barrington, in the
Berkshires, for technical assistance with an emerging community
land trust.

The setting in which Bob would live out his days in the moun-
tainous region in western Massachusetts, handy to Vermont,
Connecticut and upstate New York is nothing if not picturesque.
Redolent with Colonial and Revolutionary era history and high
culture, the Berkshires has long been a resort for both New
Yorkers and Bostonians. The area offers all the pleasures of a lush
rural summertime and the chromatic spectacle of a leaf-peeping
autumn. Visitors and those residents who can afford the tab are
regaled with natural beauty, symphonic music, modern dance,
fine dining and literary pilgrimage sites. It's almost too good to be
true — convenient to the Eastern centers of financial and cultural
power, distant enough to maintain its own character.

With uplands cloaked in hardwood forests and river valleys that
have for more than three centuries accommodated villages, small

towns, small farms and some manufacturing (water-powered at first), the Berkshires is an entrancing place. The modern community life of the region was painted into American iconography by Norman Rockwell, who lived and worked in Lenox. It has proved to be an amenable setting for the programs of the E. F. Schumacher Society.

Originally Swann and Witt meant their move to the area to be temporary. Soon enough, though, Bob was transforming a garage into a home on the newly formed Community Land Trust in the Southern Berkshires' first parcel in South Egremont. The house perches on the north slope of Jug End Mountain and overlooks the Housatonic River Valley.[3] High up, it commands a storybook view of an orchard and a meadow sloping away and opening out to low dark ranges of mountains beyond.

One of the first things Swann and Witt did after taking up residence on Jug End Mountain was to start a community economics study group that included some of the parties to the land trust, among others. The group's text was Rudolf Steiner's philosophical *World Economy*,[4] but the group meetings became a crucible for strategizing the practical work ahead.[5]

Swann got another fateful call to service that year. Led by Satish Kumar, editor of the English magazine *Resurgence*, a group of E. F. Schumacher's friends — the publisher Ian Baldwin, the philosophical biologist David Ehrenfeld, Hazel Henderson and longtime friend John McClaughry — prevailed on Bob to start an E. F. Schumacher Society in the United States.[6] Kumar, a former Jain monk and follower of Vinoba Bhave, had, not long after Schumacher's death, created such a society in England. Its purpose was to present annual lectures by distinguished thinkers to promote and advance the kind of social and economic wisdom expressed in *Small Is Beautiful*.

Such lectures became part of the American E. F. Schumacher Society's program also, but from the beginning Swann, the Society's president, and Witt, the Executive Director, wanted the organization to do hands-on local economic development as well. So began the culminating years of Swann's life. In a new home, with a partner who shared his passion for economic reform and the help of an organization whose namesake's wisdom conduced to a local focus, Bob Swann continued to pioneer what James Robertson, the British writer and economic consultant, called "a new third sector, which is neither private nor public in the conventional sense — a self-reliant community sector."[7]

When Bob and Susan began the Schumacher Society, they were handweaving themselves a roomy tent. An undated early brochure declares that "The purpose of the E. F. Schumacher Society is to promote the ideas inherent in the decentralist tradition and to implement them in practical programs for local self-reliance."[8] Accordingly the Schumacher Society in the US has functioned as a storefront for effecting Bob's and Susan's ideas about community and regional economics in the Southern Berkshires. Swann continued to write and to think through the means of community economics, among them currency issue. Borsodi's 1972 Exeter Experiment had demonstrated the acceptability of a stable commodity-backed currency and the utility of involving local banks in its exchange and circulation. Written in the wake of the late 1970s' rampant inflation, and envisioning whole, local systems that connected land trusts, renewable energy development and a currency in the form of notes backed by electrical or cordwood energy, Swann's 1981 paper "Towards an Economy of Permanence" reads like a template for survival today.

The problem? "Our lives are controlled, or governed, by a system over which we have little or no control and do not understand." Bob wrote, "...we have accepted unconsciously a system of money and banking and we are asleep in our relationship to it."[9] Waking up we may discover that as Swann put it, "money may be designed to perform in different ways with different objectives."

Swann anticipated the failure of the "dollar system" and advocated a new money system that would allow communities to do more than merely survive through barter and labor exchange. The specifications for such a system were that it should be consistent with customary practices; be redeemable in real goods of everyday value; be a universal measure of value though based on a local production and be controlled by the community, perhaps through a nonprofit bank.[10] The universal everyday item could be the kilowatt hour or the energy contained in a cord of wood, Swann hypothesized. As he had with community land trusts, Bob Swann became something of a dean of alternative and local currency, and the Southern Berkshires region became a laboratory for the currency and microfinance experiments launched by the Schumacher Society.

In 1981 the Schumacher Society's Annual Lecture series got underway with talks by two illustrious agrarian philosophers, Wendell Berry and Wes Jackson. Berry, a small farmer, peerless essayist, poet and novelist took "People, Land, and Community" as his topic. Jackson, a plant geneticist and cofounder of the independent Land Institute, issued a "Call for a Revolution in Agriculture." Continuing still, the Society's lectures recognize the thinkers, writers, organizers and social entrepreneurs who make up the invisible college of decentralism.

Over the decades, the lecturers have included the likes of Frances Moore Lappé, Jeremy Rifkin, Leopold Kohr, Hazel Henderson, Thomas Berry, David Orr and David Brower, Ivan Illich, Paul Hawken, Winona La Duke, Jerry Mander, Chellis Glendinning, David Korten, Amory Lovins, Cathrine Sneed, Oren Lyons and Judy Wicks. Following transcription and careful editing, the lectures are published in pamphlet form. In 1997, Hildegarde Hannum, the editor and a Schumacher Society board member, assembled a collection of the E.F Schumacher Society lectures for Yale University Press, adopting Wendell Berry's title *People, Land, and Community* for the book.[11]

In addition to all the intellectual industry of the Schumacher Society, Bob occupied himself with design and construction, helping to establish Community Builders, a worker-owned building cooperative. Its structure was influenced by Bob's understanding of the Mondragon producer cooperatives in the Basque region of Northern Spain.[12] The business grew from three to eleven members over its brief life until the stock market crash of 1987 trounced real estate in the region.

On the land trust property on Jug End Road, a few hundred yards from the home that Bob built for Susan and himself, Bob was commissioned to design and build a dance studio. He invoked Frank Lloyd Wright's design techniques to create a lofty yet intimate structure. The low-ceilinged entryway opens out to a large gracious space, naturally illuminated with clerestory windows and situated to take advantage of winter sun for warmth. Thanks to a local logger named Charlie Wyman, Bob was able to use local and recycled lumber from an old camp in the vicinity to create the building.[13] When several years later the owner moved on, the E. F. Schumacher Society acquired the building to house its offices and its decentralist library.

Roughly contemporary with the construction of the dance studio was the week-long first Seminar on Tools for Community Economic Transformation, one of several such to be organized by the Schumacher Society and jointly sponsored by the Intermediate Technology Development Group (ITDG) and the Durruti Institute. Bob was one of a triumvirate of leaders of the seminar, explaining the workings and implications of community land trusts and adding his ideas on community banking. The Australian businessman Shann Turnbull, an exponent of *social capitalism* (new arrangements for individual and community control of productive assets, social services and credit) and George Benello, also a businessman and a leading expert on worker-managed industries, were the two other wise men.[14] Although they didn't dwell on it, economic crisis as evidenced by high unemployment, drastic technological change and the dubiousness (even then) of high finance were backdrops to the discussions.

ITDG's Ward Morehouse saw two themes running through the seminar: "an emphasis on self-management and self-financing as a significant alternative to present dependence on centralized systems of financing, organizations, and control" and "painstaking attention to the practical details — rooted in real experience — of translating the social visions underlying these ideas into concrete reality."[15]

Community self-responsibility and the necessity for rigor in the realization of ideas have yet to find a big public, but they are the hard truths at the foundation of the Schumacher Society's programs. When it comes to things as tangible as land and money the paperwork ordaining the innovative forms — leasehold agreements for community land trusts, for instance — must be exact and evolved. The practical details involve working relationships with local businesses and institutions, like banks, that don't traffic in good intentions.

The Self-Help Association for a Regional Economy or SHARE program, whose collateralized microlending program Witt and Swann conceived, exemplified this practical and participatory approach. Its purpose was meeting first-time borrower's needs for credit to build small, productive, ecologically sound enterprises. One of the program's criteria was that applicants for SHARE loans had to have tried to get bank loans but been turned down. SHARE worked by what Susan dubbed "the grandmother principle." SHARE members would open savings accounts of $100 or more at a local savings bank, in effect becoming grandmothers cosigning loans. Those deposits would be pooled for the purpose of making small low-interest loans to applicants vetted by SHARE's elected board, working at a scale of lending — the range was from $500 to $3,000[16] — regarded as unprofitable by most banks.

As Bob explained to a reporter from the *Christian Science Monitor*, "The scale of financial institutions does not work for the creation of small businesses on a regional level.... All we've done is create an economic institution complementing the small business in this area."[17]

The program's successes generated a bumper crop of stories — knitting machines bought to increase a cottage garment industry, commercial grade equipment that allowed a goat dairy to manufacture cheese and a barn for a horse-logger's team. By helping to organize SHARE as a first step towards creating an independent local economy, the Schumacher Society was, wrote Bob, "building a base, a constituency of depositors in the community and confidence in the community — as well as developing a strong working relationship with the local banks, merchants, and farmers in the area."[18] In time interest rates fell. During the Clinton administration banks were urged to reinvest in their communities, so SHARE's low cost productive loans were no longer needed, and their accounts were closed.[19]

With the SHARE program and with the Community Land Trust of the Southern Berkshires, Swann and Witt were doing something more than advocating policy change. They were establishing new practices — and enhancing the community. Although Bob had an intelligent critique of banking, finance and monetary issue, he was, wisely, not an antagonist. Nor was Susan. The Gandhian wisdom was to build the alternative, involve people, do self-help. Not just a proving ground, laboratory or case study, the Southern Berkshires was now their home.

An ounce of practice, worth a pound of theory, takes a ton of patience. In the endeavor to develop a living local economy it turns out that ideology is not a very useful tool. Neither is rhetoric — although stories can be. Witt's innate literary sensibility attuned her to observing and retelling the stories that illustrated the workings of their novel small economic institutions. In this way, among others, she helped bring Bob's thinking to earth, working with him and very much *in* the town of Great Barrington to birth programs with the local community rather than upon it.

At the same time, and all along, the Schumacher Society's lectures and seminars kept stirring the pot of decentralist thinking, certainly not neglecting the importance of ideas and inspiration. The big thinkers of smallness had their work to do also. In 1983, the year SHARE was launched, the Schumacher Society lectures were given by Jane Jacobs, who spoke on "The Economy of Regions,"[20] and Kirkpatrick Sale who gave an introduction to bioregionalism titled "Mother of All."[21]

Among the advantages of a community land trust is the ability to develop careful land use plans for a variety of parcels and purposes. The CLT in the Southern Berkshires now dedicated itself to making land available to year round residents for agriculture, housing and cottage industry. Its strategy: purchase land and lease it to residents at the lowest possible rate.[22]

Although he was approaching his 70s, Bob was still active as a builder and enjoying the work. A project came up that involved the Community Land Trust of the Southern Berkshires and the Community Builders co-op, along with some of the Schumacher Society's staunchest supporters, in the creation of affordable housing. The project, called Forest Row, served a town where a boom market in second homes priced dwellings beyond the means of moderate-income locals.

For the Forest Row affordable housing project, the CLT was able to purchase a wooded, 21-acre piece of what had been a 125-acre mink farm just outside of Great Barrington. The land use plan clustered the housing on five acres, leaving the rest open for the residents — including the winged and four-legged — to enjoy.[23] Bob designed the multi-unit housing, gleaning an idea for the development's quadraplexes from an unfinished design by Frank Lloyd Wright. The official dedication of the project, blessed by a bishop, was in July of 1987.[24]

This was all happening back in the days when mortgage money was tight and down payments of as much as 30% of the purchase price of the residence might be required.[25] The prices of the various units were considerably lower than the region's average, but in order to bring home ownership within reach of moderate-income, year-round Berkshire residents the CLT had to start a revolving loan fund so as to provide second mortgages. This Fund for Affordable Housing attracted low-interest social investment money from individuals who saw it as a worthy cause.[26]

The Forest Row project was no ordinary real estate deal. It was strenuous, innovative and designed to help build a stable community rather than maximize profit. The home buyers were consciously forgoing any speculative increase to the value of their homes, for the trust owned the land upon which the dwellings were built. It retained the first option to buy them back at their current replacement cost.[27] Every aspect of the Forest Row Project — from the careful democracy of the land trust's organization to the construction cooperative, to the revolving loan fund as social investment vehicle — was of Bob Swann's design.

As the Schumacher Society's executive director Susan Witt played a critical part in the realization of this and all of the Community Land Trust in the Southern Berkshires and Schumacher Society projects, doing some heavy lifting, sharing in the larger vision, supplying tremendous determination and a community organizer's positive zeal. As the economy changed and the land trust sought to change the resale restriction, Susan fought for it. She became "the nonprofit developer," finding financing for the project.[28]

While they were working on these sizeable financial propositions Swann and Witt were poor as church mice. The daily life of such mom and pop nonprofits has a vicarage austerity. There's an inescapable dependence on alms. But though the means may have been slender, the style was tasteful. Bob's buildings — the house where he and Susan lived and the studio building across the way — are appealing. There are varied spaces within them and a cordial simplicity. The Schumacher Society's stationery and publications are embellished with folkway medallions drawn by Martha Shaw, their motifs alluding to good work, agrarian bounty and the New England woodland. The prose emanating from Susan and Bob's collaboration — in newsletters, funding pleas and information — was clear and compelling, with the ring of serious purpose. There were times when, to keep the Society afloat, Susan was selling off a valuable collection of paintings, but there was no public show of desperation. There also were some awful times in Bob and Susan's relationship, some years of real suffering, but they abated. The strife receded from significance as the work went on because, as Bob remarked in quite another context, "the ideas were so much bigger than the people."[29]

In 1988, Bob articulated the reasons for a decentralization of currency issue in a Schumacher Society lecture titled "The Need for Local Currencies." "I am not a specialist in monetary economics, but I have studied money for many years," he said,[30] and went on to explain some of the dysfunctions of centralized banking and currency issue in terms of some basic precepts that are acutely relevant today.

"As industrialization grew [in the 19th century], the need for larger amounts of money to finance the large industries with their 'economies of scale' grew also. Huge sums of money also meant the need for big banks, and big banks need many depositors. The greatest concentration of depositors was in the cities."[31] The upshot was agglomerations of banks and a flow of deposits from rural regions to the cities, resulting in a dearth of money to develop diversified rural economies. "The result is extreme disparity between different regions of the country," Bob said.

Swann harked back to the Jeffersonian era of "free banking" when small local banks issued their own currency and "provided the money and credit for small farmers to produce and sell their goods."[32] These bankers "were dealing in a personal way," and could make loans based on character when there was no collateral. "Perhaps most importantly, this local currency…could only circulate in a limited regional area…. Small businesses did not have to compete for credit with larger businesses in other places as they do now that deposits are pooled in the urban areas."

The arguments against there being a plethora of local banks and currencies then and now, said Swann, were that sometimes such banks were run by scoundrels and could fail. "The feeling was that such abuses could be controlled if money were issued centrally.... *But decentralization and diversity have the benefit of preventing large-scale failure*" (my italics).[33]

Bob was giving this lecture at the moment of the savings and loan banking bailout which foreshadowed and paved the way for the multibillion-dollar bailouts of the end of the first decade of the 21st century. A colossal bank failure was imminent with billions added to the national debt. The centralized financial edifices were propped up, and the large-scale failure was put off for a while.

In his talk Swann laid out precepts for local currency, addressing the core issue of banking: confidence. "What, then, will provide confidence in regionally issued currency?"[34] Redemption in a locally produced commodity, Swann thought then. Quite as important would be the structure of the issuing organization. It should be a nonprofit, so as to "not line any individual pocket," it should be democratic, with open membership and an elected board and "Its policy should be to create new credit for short term, productive purposes only.... Clearly this is not inflationary." Swann also thought that regional banks should be free of government control and hence from political motivations.[35]

"Finally," he said, "and this is the newest element which must be introduced into banking, is the use of both social and ecological criteria in making loans...."[36] That particular vision remains to be realized although in a serious depression "such [local] currencies will again become necessities" as they had in the 1930s, Bob thought.

In the following year, and without the serious depression, SHARE encouraged the creation of some engaging local scrips.

Their acclaim helped trigger the development of a spate of local currencies around the US.

Deli Dollars came first. The owner of a popular local eatery in Great Barrington was unable to borrow the few thousand dollars he needed to move and later finance a renovation. Swann and Witt suggested a self-financing scrip. Supportive customers would purchase discounted Deli Dollars redeemable for edibles at a specified time in the future. The idea was a success. The relocation was financed, and in the meantime the Deli Dollars started behaving like money — passing from hand to hand. Some Deli Dollars even found their way into the First Congregational Church's collection plate.[37] SHARE helped a few other small businesses — including two farm stands, a general store and a Japanese restaurant — launch self-financing scrips. Their flourishing drew significant media attention throughout the region, the nation and beyond. There even was coverage in the *International Herald Tribune*. The news piqued the imagination of a social entrepreneur named Paul Glover. Glover traveled to the Berkshires for a week-long tutorial in monetary issue with Bob Swann and some serious research on the theory and history of regional scrip issue at the E. F. Schumacher Library.[38] Glover then repaired to Ithaca, New York, where in 1991 he launched *Ithaca Hours*, the local currency that by its success acted like a sourdough starter to ferment local currency initiatives all over the US.

It was also in 1991 that I first met Bob Swann and Susan Witt, through our mutual friend Hildegarde Hannum. The thought was that I might do some writing about the Schumacher Society. I traveled to Jug End Mountain and was billeted in the Library building, which has a few pleasantly monastic cells to accommodate visiting scholars. It was high summer and beautiful. It was, alas, a time when Susan and Bob's relationship appeared to be rocky. Still they both and each did their best to help me understand what the Society was up to even as they tended to their projects. By then, Bob was in his early 70s, still working construction and playing tennis.

The local currency experiments continued in 1992, with the issue of a downtown trade dollar called Berkshares, whose success was helped by the fact that the diligent, dynamic Witt had been elected to the presidency of the Great Barrington Rotary Club. By this time the E. F. Schumacher Society was well established (if not well-heeled). It was receiving "uninterrupted international press coverage."[39] It could pursue its variety of works from the ongoing lectures and occasional conferences to its support of the Community Land Trust in the Southern Berkshires expansion and the diversification and the development of the library. In 1994 E. F. Schumacher's widow conveyed his personal library of books and papers to the library, a keystone gift.[40]

The arrival of E. F. Schumacher's library at an unheated building necessitated a flurry of remodeling and shelf-building activity from Bob. In retrospect, it was evident that Bob's spatial memory was beginning to falter at this time, for the shelves were uneven and things were going unfinished. "That was really sad and confusing,"

E.F.Schumacher Society

Bob Swann in the Schumacher Society library

said Susan.[41] It was the onset of Bob's old age and the end of his career as a builder. His mind still held, though, and he was present and available for conversation and discussion with the young people who were finding their ways to the Schumacher Society to learn about the practices and philosophies of local economics. A continuous stream of volunteers and interns also were treated to Bob's company and low-key instruction. Susan shouldered all the responsibility for the Society's daily direction.

In the summer of 1996, a "real undertaking" was accomplished — a first annual Decentralist Conference, which, among its other accomplishments, brought together most of the new money thinkers and doers like Paul Glover and Tom Greco, whose book *New Money for Healthy Communities*[42] was a comprehensive text on money and monetary issue for the common good. Bob participated in the conference as a recognized pioneer and source of many of the ideas behind new grass-roots monetary reform initiatives.[43] A second Decentralist Conference was held the following year, at which Bob and Schumacher Society resource coordinator Erika Levasseur made a presentation on Ralph Borsodi as an "Unsung Decentralist Hero of the 20th Century." An appreciable amount of this conference's program also was devoted to the subject of local currency.

With the launch of a website in 1997 the Schumacher Society and its outreach moved swiftly into the computer age. The speedy new internet mode of communication was not for Bob. The shift left him out of much conversation on the issues and apart from the day-to-day business of the Schumacher Society. Still keen to communicate his ideas and experience, Bob began writing his autobiography.

For her part Susan, with the Community Land Trust of the Southern Berkshires, was putting together a complicated land deal to acquire the historic Indian Line Farm. This was where the late Robyn Van En had begun the first Community Supported Agriculture (CSA) program in the US, seeding an idea that has been taken up by hundreds of small farmers since. Months before planting time, CSA farmers presell shares of their produce directly to consumers. This brings in cash at a lean time and involves the patrons with the farms, for their weekly or biweekly shares consist of whatever and however much can be prudently harvested at the time.

The Land Trust sought to acquire Indian Line Farm and lease most of the land to a young farming couple, who would purchase and own the structures on it. A portion of the land was protected by a conservation easement held by the local Nature Conservancy chapter. Thus there were several parties involved in working out the funding and the details of the acquisition, the easement, the details of the lease and the farm management plan, creating a new model for farm tenure and a set of documents to ratify it. "We came up against stumbling blocks one after another," said Susan. "We just needed pure stamina to meet them all."[44]

Meanwhile, Bob's health was beginning to erode. In the summer of 1999, he was quite sick and hallucinating as a result of a severe electrolyte imbalance. He was in and out of hospitals and nursing homes until at length, it was discovered that he had colon cancer. He underwent the necessary surgery. The illness left him at times bewildered and in need of a great deal of care. By March of 2000, it was clear that Bob needed more attention and a more regular schedule than Susan, with her responsibilities at the helm of the Schumacher Society, could possibly provide.

Happily, Bob and a longtime friend and neighbor, Johnny Root, were able to scout around the region to find a place that would suit him. They discovered Cameron House, a publicly subsidized, assisted living facility in a nicely renovated old brick school building in Lenox, some 18 miles north of South Egremont. Bob moved into a sunny, roomy apartment there to live out his remaining days.[45]

It was at Cameron House that I visited with, and interviewed, Bob, first in March and then in August and early September of 2001. For my part that time with Bob was a mission, trying to divine his springs and sources, to understand the man who had lived the life. For Bob those visits offered companionship and conversation. They were welcome if perhaps baffling, for at that point Bob had already done his writing. It wasn't immediately clear to either of us what a joint endeavor might accomplish, other than a publishable book.

At our meetings Bob Swann was vital and warm, always interested in new possibilities and in the work of kindred thinkers. Futuristic forms of energy generation, like cold fusion, had captured his imagination. He was reading and expounding upon works on monetary issue by James Robertson and Margrit Kennedy. Although his intellect was vital as ever his memory was deteriorating, so his mental processes could be patchy. My interviews wound up covering much the same ground he had in his autobiography. If they disclosed anything more than Bob's own recollections, it was his consistency of character, his working wisdom and the depth of his understanding of the history he'd helped to make.

During that August I accompanied Bob to some unprogrammed, or silent, Quaker meetings for worship. He attended them as much for the society of friends as for spiritual endeavor. Making arrangements over the telephone for our first such outing, I reminded Bob that I'd be coming that Sunday to attend the meeting with him and to listen for the still small voice within. He said he'd been listening for a long time but hadn't heard it yet. I remonstrated that he seemed to have been living his life entirely by his own inner light. "It's been fun," he did admit. In all our conversations Bob voiced very few regrets. His graciousness and goodwill cast an amiable glow about him.

The horrible events of September 11, 2001 provided a terminal punctuation to my sojourn in the Berkshires. Under that cloud of shock, sorrow and a outrage-fanned patriotism, I headed home to Michigan to wrest a book out of the materials of Bob's works and days. In 2002 when the anniversary of 9/11 rolled around, the staff at Cameron House, rather than reliving the attacks and retailing the destruction, transmuted it into an event to celebrate Bob's life. They held a party complete with food, music and old people dancing to the tune "Tiger Paw,"[46] along with fulsome praises of the honoree. Bob's old friend Juanita Nelson came over from her home at the Traprock Peace Center near Deerfield, Massachusetts to join, as she put it, in "celebrating a life dedicated to a vision of a nonviolent world, to be reached only by nonviolent means."

"What is so endearing about Bob," explained Nelson, " is that he tries to be what he advocates." She concluded her tribute saying that Bob was a grand example of the Peacemakers' statement that "One individual, living according to deeply held beliefs, can, in a small but significant way, begin to change the world."[47]

Not very long after that Bob was found to have metastatic cancer. He was dying. The Schumacher Society Board of Directors asked Susan to help Bob prepare a final letter to the Society's members. Bob's ready response was not a reflection or a summation, but advice on community economics: "The most important thing for the future," he said, "will be to train several local communities in the making of productive loans so that these communities can act as models for others."[48]

The last time Bob left Cameron House for the hospital, Marj and Juanita Nelson had a final visit with Bob, at Dhyana Swann's request.[49] In his very last hours, Susan brought Bob, by ambulance, back to the house on Jug End Road. Bob Swann died at home January 13, 2003, aged 84. His body rested there for a few days before it was placed in a simple wooden casket. During the wake a hammer and measuring tape, among other objects, were placed on the casket's lid. Friends who attended wrote "The message, or so it seemed, was to let us all now get to work building the kind of world we want to live in."[50]

Bob's body was cremated. His ashes were scattered in the apple orchard at his home on Jug End Mountain.[51] A public memorial service was scheduled for February 22. As that date drew nigh, a tremendous ice storm threatened New England. Cancelling and postponing the service seemed the obvious thing to do. Yet one person traveled to Great Barrington that day despite the weather — the venerable Thomas Berry. Berry, a Passionist father, author and cultural historian, who regarded Bob Swann as "among the noblest persons I have ever known"[52] arrived at Jug End Mountain to pay his respects, ice storm notwithstanding.

The rescheduled memorial service was held March 29, 2003 at the Romanesque granite First Congregational Church on Main Street in Great Barrington. Friends and colleagues from throughout the region filled the sanctuary to share their remembrances. Bob's longtime libertarian colleague and devoted friend John McLaughry, began the sharing by describing Bob as "a friend of humanity." Juanita Nelson was there to speak, too, remembering Bob as a forerunner and perennial builder of "structures for true humanity."

Perhaps the most affecting tribute came not from old friends but from Heather Davidson, a young Schumacher Society staff member. Heather described herself as being "young enough to need a hero or two," and remarked that Bob had been "jailed for resisting what his elders asked of him when he was my age." In her appreciation Bob Swann was "a man of true practicality," propelled by a "hunger to right wrongs and empower people" ever asking "What can be done to make this better?" Although he had lived long and well, zestfully and prolifically, on that cold spring afternoon in 2003, there was a tacit echo to Heather's lament: "If only Bob had more time to teach us!"

Heather took it upon herself to distill and articulate some of the teaching she had gathered in her years of working with Bob. She thought he might say

> Surround yourself with the things you love.
> Follow your ideas until something tangible emerges.
> Use your gifts to empower others.
> Seek community and if you don't find it, build it.[53]

Endnotes

Preface and Acknowledgments
1. Robert Swann. *Peace, Civil Rights, and the Search for Community: An Autobiography (PCRSC)*. [online]. [cited 27 July 2009]. smallisbeautiful.org/about/biographies/swann_autobiography/swann_toc.html.
2. Stephanie Mills. "Bob Swann's 'Positively Dazzling Realism.'" [online]. [cited 27 July 2009]. smallisbeautiful.org/publications/mills_04.html.
3. Stephanie Mills. "Young Vigor Searching for Light: Bob Swann, Arthur Morgan, and the Pantheon of Decentralism." [online]. [cited 27 July 2009]. smallisbeautiful.org/publications/mills_swann_bio.html.

Chapter 1
1. Albert Camus. "Neither Victims nor Executioners" in *Seeds of Liberation*, ed. Paul Goodman. Braziller, 1964, p. 39.
2. Robert Swann. Interview by the author, 17 August 2001.
3. Karl Polanyi. *The Great Transformation: The Political and Economic Origins of Our Time*. 1944, reprint Beacon, 1957.
4. Susan Meeker-Lowry. *Economics as if the Earth Really Mattered: A Catalyst Guide to Socially Conscious Investing*. New Society, 1988.

Chapter 2
1. James Swann. Interview by the author, 26 March 2008.
2. Marjorie Swann Edwin. "Memories of Bob Swann." Talk given at a family memorial service, 20 November 2003.
3. *PCRSC*.
4. Ibid.
5. Robert Swann. "Paper written for Lesson No. 1 in Arthur Morgan's course on 'The Small Community.'" 15 October 1943. Arthur Morgan papers, Olive Kettering Memorial Library, Antioch College.
6. *PCRSC*.
7. Ibid.
8. Robert Swann. Interview by the author, 2 September 2001.

9. PCRSC.

10. Ibid.

11. James Swann. Interview.

12. PCRSC.

13. James Swann. Interview.

14. Robert Swann. Interview by the author, 22 March 2001.

15. PCRSC.

16. Ibid.

17. James Swann. Interview.

18. Linda Marie Delloff. "Beyond Stewardship: A Theology for Nature." Foreword to *Care of the Earth: An Environmental Resource Manual for Church Leaders*. [online]. [cited 30 June 2009]. webofcreation.org/Manuals/krause/contents.html.

19. Messiah Lutheran Church. *Church History page*. [online]. [cited 30 June 2009]. messiahlyndhurst.org.

20. Delloff. "Beyond Stewardship."

21. Edwin. "Memories."

22. Robert Swann. Interview by the author, 22 March 2001.

23. Howard Zinn. *A People's History of the United States: 1492–Present*, revised and updated edition. Harper, 1995, p. 385.

24. Robert Swann. Interview by the author, 26 August 2001.

25. PCRSC.

26. Roni Feinstein. "Lichtenstein: Seeing is Believing." *Art in America*, July 2002. [online]. [cited 30 June 2009]. findarticles.com/p/articles/mi_m1248/is_7_90/ai_88582351/?tag=content;col1.

27. Robert Swann. Interview by the author, 22 March 2001.

28. Robert Swann. Interview by Mary-Beth Raddon, 18 August 1997. E. F. Schumacher Library, photocopied typescript, p. 1.

29. PCRSC.

30. John D'Emilio. *Lost Prophet: The Life and Times of Bayard Rustin*. Free Press, 2003, pp. 43–44.

31. Robert Swann. Interview by the author, 16 August 2001.

32. Robert Swann. Interview by Mary-Beth Raddon, 18 August 1997, p. 2.

33. Robert Swann. Interview by the author, 2 September 2001.

34. PCRSC.

35. David E. Shi. *The Simple Life: Plain Living and High Thinking in American Culture*. Oxford University Press, 1985, p. 230.

36. Ibid., p. 255.

37. Joseph Kip Kosek. "Richard Gregg, Mohandas Gandhi, and the Strategy of Nonviolence." *Journal of American History*, Vol. 91 No. 4 (March 2005), p. 1346.

38. *PCRSC.*
39. Robert Swann. Interview by Mary-Beth Raddon, 18 August 1997, p. 2.
40. Robert Swann. Letter to James Swann, 4 December 1942.
41. Krishna Dutta and Andrew Robinson. *Rabindranath Tagore: The Myriad-Minded Man.* St. Martin's, 1995, p. 237.
42. Carol Swann. Interview by the author, 1 April 2004.
43. Carol Swann. "Dad, the Memorial Speech I Didn't Give." Photocopy.

Chapter 3

1. Robert Cooney and Helen Michalowski, eds. *The Power of the People: Active Nonviolence in the United States.* Peace Press, 1977, p.14.
2. Nicholas Von Hoffman. *Make-Believe Presidents: Illusions of Power from McKinley to Carter.* Pantheon, 1978, p. 157.
3. Zinn. *People's History*, p. 355.
4. Cooney and Michalowski. *Power*, p. 45.
5. Larry Gara and Lenna Mae Gara. *A Few Small Candles: War Resisters of World War II Tell Their Stories.* Kent State University, 1999, p. xi.
6. Larry Gara. Telephone conversation with the author, 10 January 2005.
7. Robert Swann. Interview by the author, 21 August 2001.
8. David Dellinger. Quoted in Gara and Gara, *Candles*, p. 30.
9. Cooney and Michalowski. *Power*, p. 93.
10. Robert Swann. Interview by the author, 17 August 2001.
11. Kosek. "Richard Gregg," p. 1324.
12. Ibid., p. 1333.
13. Richard Gregg. *The Big Idol.* Navajivan, 1963.
14. Richard Gregg. *Which Way Lies Hope?* Navajivan, 1952.
15. Richard Gregg. *The Power of Nonviolence.* Lippincott, 1934 and Schocken, 1966.
16. Kosek. "Richard Gregg," p. 1341.
17. Marian Mollin. *Radical Pacifism in Modern America: Egalitarianism and Protest.* University of Pennsylvania, 2006, p. 28.
18. Gara and Gara. *Candles*, p. xii.
19. Kosek. "Richard Gregg," p. 1341.
20. Arthur Dole. Quoted in Gara and Gara, *Candles*, p. 66.
21. Robert Swann. Interview by the author, 26 March 2001.
22. *PCRSC.*
23. William Roberts. Quoted in Gara and Gara, *Candles*, p. 157.
24. Kosek. "Richard Gregg," p. 1341.

25. Lawrence S. Wittner. *Rebels Against War: The American Peace Movement, 1941–1960.* Columbia, 1969, p. 89.

26. Robert Swann. Interview by the author, 26 March 2001.

27. MANAS Reprints Summer 1999. Flyer from MANAS reprints, 245 W. 33rd. Street, Los Angeles, CA 90007.

Chapter 4

1. Joseph Tainter. *The Collapse of Complex Societies.* Cambridge, 1988.

2. PCRSC.

3. Arthur E. Morgan. *The Small Community: Foundation of Democratic Life.* Community Service Inc., 1942 and 1984.

4. Henry Geiger. "The Community Movement" Brochure. Community Service, Inc., n.d.

5. Arthur E. Morgan. "An Open Letter to Civilian Public Service Camp Members from Arthur E. Morgan." 12 March 1942. Morgan Papers.

6. Larry Gara. Telephone conversation with the author, 10 January 2005.

7. Arthur E. Morgan. "Syllabus for Correspondence Course on The Small Community." Autumn 1943. Arthur Morgan Papers.

8. Liberty Hyde Bailey. *The Holy Earth.* Macmillan, 1915 and Christian Rural Fellowship, 1943.

9. Lewis Mumford. *The Culture of Cities.* Harcourt, 1938.

10. Peter Kropotkin. *Mutual Aid: A Factor of Evolution.* 1902; reprint with an introduction by John Hewetson, Freedom, 1987.

11. Shi. *Simple Life,* p. 236.

12. Morgan. *Small Community,* p. 63.

13. Ibid., p. 282.

14. Arthur E. Morgan. *The Long Road.* Community Service Inc., 1936 and 1962, p. 34.

15. Peter Kropotkin. *Fields, Factories and Workshops.* 1912; reprint with an introduction by Yaacov Oved, Transaction, 1993.

16. Martin A. Miller. *Kropotkin.* University of Chicago, 1976, pp. 245–246.

17. Kropotkin. *Mutual Aid,* p. 16.

18. Mumford. *Culture of Cities,* p. 11.

19. Ibid., p. 475.

20. Ibid., p. 327.

21. Edward S. Shapiro. "Decentralist Intellectuals and the New Deal." *Journal of American History,* Vol. 58 No. 4 (March 1972), p. 438.

22. Mumford. *Culture of Cities,* p. 306.

23. Robert Swann. *Résumé.* E. F. Schumacher Library, photocopy, n.d.

24. Robert Swann. Letter to James Swann, 15 September 1942.

25. Robert Swann. Letter to James Swann, 30 September 1942.

26. Robert Swann. Letter to James Swann, 4 December 1942.

27. Robert Swann. Letter to James Swann, December 1942.

28. Robert Swann. Letter to James Swann, 30 August 1943.

29. Robert Swann. Letter to James Swann, 22 September 1943.

30. Robert Swann. Letter to James Swann, 18 January 1944.

31. Robert Swann. Letter to James Swann, 22 February 1944.

32. J. Russell Smith. *Tree Crops: A Permanent Agriculture.* 1929, reprint Island, 1987.

33. Robert Swann. Letter to James Swann, 2 April 1944.

34. Robert Swann. Letter to James Swann, 21 April 1944.

35. Robert Swann. Letter to James Swann, 5 May 1944.

36. Robert Swann. Letter to James Swann, 5 May 1944.

37. Robert Swann. Letter to James Swann, 18 August 1944.

38. Robert Swann. Letter to James Swann, 22 September 1943.

39. Robert Swann. Letter to James Swann, 22 February 1944.

Chapter 5

1. Mollin. *Radical Pacifism*, p. 26.

2. Marjorie Swann Edwin. Interview by the author, 29 March 2004.

3. Robert Swann and Ray Olds. Conversation with the author, 21 August 2001.

4. Edwin. Interview.

5. Ibid.

6. Edwin. "Memories."

7. PCRSC.

8. Robert Swann. Letter to Arthur Morgan, 27 September 1944. Morgan Papers.

9. Robert Swann. Letter to Arthur Morgan, 27 November 1944. Morgan Papers.

10. Robert Swann. Letter to Arthur Morgan, 30 March 1945. Morgan Papers.

11. Robert Swann. Letter to Arthur Morgan, 27 October 1945. Morgan Papers.

12. Robert Swann Letter to Arthur Morgan, 25 April 1946; Arthur Morgan. Letter to Robert Swann, 6 May 1946. Morgan Papers.

13. Robert Swann. Letter to Arthur Morgan, 15 May 1946; Arthur Morgan. Letter to Robert and Marjorie Swann, 18 May 1946; Marjorie and Robert Swann. Letter to Arthur Morgan, 20 May 1946; Arthur Morgan. Letter to Robert and Marjorie Swann, 22 May 1946; Robert and Marjorie Swann. Letter to Arthur Morgan,

26 May 1946; Robert Swann. Letter to Arthur Morgan, 7 June 1946. Morgan Papers.

14. Robert Swann and Raymond Olds. Conversation.

15. *PCRSC.*

16. Robert Swann. Interview by the author, 22 March 2001.

17. Robert Swann. Interview by the author, 2 September 2001.

18. Robert Swann. Letter to Arthur Morgan, 26 February 1948; Robert Swann. Letter to Morris Bean, 26 February 1948; Robert Swann. Letter to Murray D. Lincoln, 19 February 1948; Robert Swann. Memo to Messrs. Stewart, Alexander, Bean and Mercer, 24 February 1948. Morgan Papers.

19. Joyce F. Weinbrecht. "From Time to Time." *The Hastings Banner*, 1998, typescript. Circle Pines Center Archives.

20. Robert Swann. Letter to Arthur Morgan, 26 February 1948. Morgan Papers.

21. Cooney and Michalowski. *Power*, p. 111.

22. August Meier and Elliot Rudwick. *CORE: A Study in the Civil Rights Movement, 1942–1968.* Oxford, 1973, p. 44.

23. Wittner. *Rebels*, pp. 227–228.

24. Robert Swann and Raymond Olds. Conversation

25. Marjorie Swann Edwin. Telephone conversation with the author, 13 July 2009.

26. Mollin. *Radical Pacifism*, pp. 24–25.

27. Paul Salstrom. Note to the author, 10 August 2009.

28. Juanita Nelson. Interview by the author, 29 March 2003.

29. Meier and Rudwick. *CORE*, p. 44.

30. Mollin. *Radical Pacifism*, p. 33.

31. Ibid., p. 41.

32. Ibid., p. 57.

33. Juanita Nelson. "A Matter of Freedom" in *Seeds of Liberation*, ed. Paul Goodman. Braziller, 1964.

34. James Swann. Interview.

35. Lois G. Runeman, ed. *Anthology–1944: First Fruits: A Collection of Creative Works by Members and Friends of Circle Pines Center.* Circle Pines Center, 1944, p. 8.

36. "Extracts from *Pine Needles*, July 10–July 17, 1938." Carbon copy, p. 15. Circle Pines Center Archives.

37. William A. Knox. Letter to Mrs. Ruth Sumner, 19 February 1963. Circle Pines Center Archives.

38. *PCRSC.*

39. Runeman. *Anthology.*

40. *PCRSC.*

41. Robert Swann. Interview by the author, 17 August 2001.

42. *PCRSC.*
43. Edwin. Interview.
44. Edwin. "Memories."
45. Judy Swann. Interview by the author, 7 April 2004.
46. Robert Swann. *Résumé.*
47. Wittner. *Rebels,* p. 48.
48. Walter P. Reuther Library. *Worker's Defense League Records.* [online]. [cited 9 July 2009]. reuther.wayne.edu/node/3178.
49. "Morris Milgram" in Frances Carol Locher, ed. *Contemporary Authors, Volumes 73–76.* Gale, 1978, p. 433.
50. Wittner. *Rebels,* p. 202.
51. Jhan Robbins and June Robbins. "You Are a Bad Mother." *Redbook,* August 1960.
52. Robert Swann. Letters to Marjorie Swann, 22 August 1959, 31 August 1959, 18 October 1959, 6 December 1959, 22 December 1959 and four undated.
53. Dhyana (née Barbara) Swann. Interview by the author, 28 March 2004.
54. Marjorie Swann Edwin. Interview.
55. Dhyana (née Barbara) Swann. Interview.
56. Judy Swann. Interview by the author, 7 April 2004.
57. Carol Swann. E-mail to the author, 7 June 2009.
58. Carol Swann. Interview.
59. Scott Swann. Interview by the author, 24 April 2004.
60. Carol Swann. Interview.
61. Scott Swann. Interview.

Chapter 6
1. Cooney and Michalowski. *Power,* p. 129.
2. Ibid., p. 133.
3. Paul Salstrom. Letter to the author, 23 October 2007.
4. Brad Lyttle. Untitled typescript dated 11 October 1998, p. 1. E. F. Schumacher Library.
5. Ibid., p. 6.
6. Ibid., p. 7.
7. Ibid., p. 19.
8. Richard Anthony. "Hard Times Down on the Voluntown Farm." *The Rhode Islander,* 15 November 1970, p. 11.
9. Voluntown Peace Trust website. *About VPT.* [online]. [cited July 10, 2009]. voluntownpeacetrust.org/history.html.
10. Anthony. "Hard Times," p. 16.
11. Paul Salstrom. Letter to the author, 23 October 2007.
12. Ibid.

13. Voluntown Peace Trust website. *About VPT*.

14. Ibid.

15. Marjorie Swann. *Decade of Nonviolence: Through the Years with New England CNVA*. New England Committee for Nonviolent Action, n.d.

16. Anthony. "Hard Times," p. 9.

17. Joel Sekeres. "Voluntown Hostile to Pacifists." *Providence Sunday Journal*, 22 September 1968.

18. Ibid.

19. Anthony. "Hard Times," p. 9.

20. Ibid., p. 11.

21. Scott Swann. Interview.

22. Cooney and Michalowski. *Power*, p. 116.

23. Sankar Ghose. *Leaders of Modern India*. Allied Publishers Private Ltd., 1980, pp. 374 ff.

24. Robert Swann. "Direct Action and Constructive Program." *MANAS*, Vol. XIV No. 10, 8 March 1961.

25. Frederic Kelly. "The Voluntown Pacifists." *New Haven Register* Sunday Supplement, circa 1966. Photocopy, n.d.

26. Dennis Weeks. "The Haywood Handicrafters League: Go South, Young Man!" *Liberation*, September 1963, pp. 17–19.

27. Paul Salstrom. Letter to the author, 8 January 2005.

28. Cooney and Michalowski. *Power*, p. 137.

29. D'Emilio. *Lost Prophet*, p. 314.

30. Robert Swann. Letter to Paul Salstrom, 4 September 1962.

31. Robert Swann. Letter to Paul Salstrom, 4 March 1963.

32. Jane Jacobs. *The Death and Life of Great American Cities*. Vintage, 1961.

33. Robert Swann. "Action for Peace, Freedom, and Community." *MANAS*, Vol. XVII No. 1, 1 January 1964.

34. Ibid.

35. Marjorie Swann quoted in *MANAS*, Vol. XVII No. 20, 19 May 1965.

36. Ibid.

37. Robert Swann. Interview by the author, 3 August 2001.

38. Paul Salstrom. Letter to the author, 6 October 2007.

39. Gorham Munson. *Aladdin's Lamp: The Wealth of the American People*. Creative Age, 1945, p. 94.

40. Ibid., p. 114.

41. Ibid., p. 121.

42. Ibid., p. 132.

43. Ibid., p. 188.

44. Ibid., p. 220.

45. Robert Swann. Interview by Shann Turnbull, typescript, n.d. E. F. Schumacher Library.

46. Paul Salstrom. "Coming Over the Hill — Land Trusts: Who Was Responsible." *Green Revolution*, September 1975.

47. Harry Cleaver. "Socialism" in *The Development Dictionary*, Wolfgang Sachs, ed. Zed Books, 1992.

48. Salstrom. "Coming Over the Hill," p. 6.

49. Carolyn Kinsey. "Interview with Dr. Ralph Borsodi." *Mother Earth News*, No. 26, March-April 1974. [online]. [cited 10 July 2009]. soilandhealth.org/03sov/0303critic/Brsdi.intrvw/The Plowboy -Borsodi Interview.htm.

50. Porter Sargent website — About Us — History. *F. Porter Sargent (1915–1975)*. [online]. [cited 20 July 2009]. portersargent.com.

51. Robert Swann. Interview by the author, 31 August 2001.

52. Shi. *Simple Life*, p. 226.

53. Ibid., p. 227.

54. Ralph Borsodi. *This Ugly Civilization*. Simon and Schuster, 1929.

55. Ralph Borsodi. *Flight from the City: The Story of a New Way to Family Security*. Harper and Row, 1933, reprint 1965.

56. Henry George. *Progress and Poverty: An Inquiry into the Cause of Industrial Depression and of Increase of Want with Increase of Wealth*. 1880, reprint Modern Library, 1938.

57. Robert Heilbroner. *The Worldly Philosophers: The Lives, Times, and Ideas of the Great Economic Thinkers*, 6th ed. Simon and Schuster, 1986, p. 188.

58. John Ferrell. "This Land Was Made for You and Me: Finding New Roots in the Past." *RAIN*, June 1982.

59. John Blackmore. "Community Trusts Offer a Hopeful Way Back to the Land." *Smithsonian*, Vol. 9 No. 3, June 1978.

60. Shi. *Simple Life*, p. 242.

61. Ibid. p. 245.

62. Paul Salstrom. "Minutes of the Conference on Plans for the International Independence Institute." *Venture*, No. 3, 26 August 1966.

63. Salstrom. "Coming Over the Hill," p. 6.

64. Marjorie Swann. "Decade."

65. Anthony. "Hard Times," p. 9.

66. Marta Daniels. Interview by the author, 6 January 2009.

Chapter 7

1. Ghose. *Modern India*, p. 290.

2. *MANAS*, Vol. XIX No. 30, 27 July 1966.

3. Ibid.

4. Robert Swann. "The Economics of Peace." *Catholic Worker*, January 1967.

5. Ibid.

6. Ibid.

7. Ibid.

8. *PCRSC.*

9. *MANAS*, Vol. XXI No. 51, 18 December 1968.

10. Robert Swann, Erick Hansch, Shimon Gottschalk and Edward Webster. *The Community Land Trust: A Guide to a Model for Land Tenure in America.* Center for Community Economic Development, 1972, pp. 16–17.

11. Swann et al. *Community Land Trust.*

12. Swann et al. *Community Land Trust*, p. 17.

13. Ibid., p. 23.

14. Robert Swann. "Rural Credit as a Key to Development: A Report on a Mexican Experiment." *Green Revolution*, September 1976.

15. Blackmore. "Community Trusts Offer a Hopeful Way."

16. Robert Swann. Interview by Mary Beth Raddon.

17. Robert Swann. "Rural Credit as a Key to Development."

18. "To Friends of the International Independence Institute." June 1970. Photocopy, E. F. Schumacher Library.

19. Robert Swann. "A New World Bank and Currency Proposal." ca. 1975. Photocopy, E. F. Schumacher Library.

20. Ibid.

21. Sam Adams. "Remembrance for Bob Swann." Delivered at a memorial service, Great Barrington, Massachusetts, 29 March 2003.

22. E. F. Schumacher. *Small Is Beautiful: Economics as if People Mattered.* Harper & Row, 1973.

23. Robert Swann. "The Community Land Trust" in Peter Barnes, ed. *The People's Land.* Rodale, 1975, pp. 215–216.

24. Salstrom. "Coming Over the Hill," p. 6.

25. Dorothy Day. "Economics: On Pilgrimage — September 1974." *Catholic Worker*, September 1974. [online]. [cited 15 July 2009]. catholicworker.org/dorothyday/daytext.cfm?TextID=543.

26. Ibid.

27. Robert Swann. "Energy, PetroCurrency and the World's Future." n.d. Photocopy, E. F. Schumacher Library.

28. Robert Swann. "A World Currency Based on Community Land Trust Resources." n.d. Photocopy, E. F. Schumacher Library.

29. Robert Swann. "Proposal for a Village Monetary System Based on Trusteeship." n.d. Photocopy, E. F. Schumacher Library.

30. Robert Swann. "Community Land Trust: A New Ownership Approach?" *Catholic Rural Life*, Vol 25 No. 3, March 1976.

31. Robert Swann. "Land Trusts as a Part of a Threefold Strategy for Regional Integration" n.d. Photocopy, E. F. Schumacher Library.

32. Robert Swann. "Appropriate Technology and New Approaches to Ownership" n.d. Photocopy, E. F. Schumacher Library.

33. Robert Swann. "Rural Credit as a Key to Development."

34. Robert Swann. "To Friends and Associates of the III: Meeting with Prince Mohamad Al-Faisal of Saudi Arabia." 1 December 1975. Photocopy, E. F. Schumacher Library.

35. Terry Mollner. *The Story of Bob Swann's Relationship with Launching of the Socially Responsible Investment Industry.* [online]. [cited 15 July 2009]. trusteeship.org/Articles/Trusteeship_Bob Swann_SocialResponsibility.html.

36. Robert Swann. Interview by the author, 30 August 2001.

37. Susan Witt. "Question for Susan." E-mail to Gary Lamb, 9 December 2008.

38. Susan Witt. "Stirred by Promise and Necessity" in *Robert Swann: Tributes*. E. F. Schumacher Society, 2003.

39. "Susan Witt" in John Mongillo and Bibi Booth, eds. *Environmental Activists*. Greenwood, 2001, p. 298.

40. Institute for Community Economics. *Loan Fund.* [online]. [cited 15 July 2009]. iceclt.org/loanfund/.

41. National Community Land Trust Network. *Foreclosure.* [online]. [cited 30 July 2009]. cltnetwork.org/index .php?fuseaction=Blog.dspBlogPost&postID=36.

42. Susan Witt. Phone conversation with the author, 15 January 2005.

43. Peter Barnes. *Who Owns the Land? A Primer on Land Reform in the USA.* Center for Rural Studies, 1976; Daniel Zwerdling. *Workplace Democracy: A Guide to Workplace Ownership, Participation & Self-Management Experiments in the United States & Europe.* Harper, 1980.

44. Robert Swann. Interview by the author, 30 August 2001.

Chapter 8

1. PCRSC.

2. Susan Witt. Phone conversation with the author, n.d.

3. Mongillo and Booth. *Environmental Activists*, p. 298.

4. Rudolf Steiner. *World Economy: The Formation of a Science of World-Economics — a Series of Fourteen Lectures*, Rev. ed. Rudolf Steiner, 1949.

5. Susan Witt. "Question for Susan."

6. Nancy Jack Todd. "Introduction" in Hildegarde Hannum, ed. *People, Land, and Community*. Yale, 1997, p. 7.

7. Ward Morehouse, ed. *Building Sustainable Communities: Tools and*

Concepts for Self-Reliant Economic Change. Bootstrap, 1989, back cover copy.

8. Brochure. E. F. Schumacher Society, n.d. E. F. Schumacher Library.
9. Robert Swann. "The Place of a Local Currency in a World Economy: Towards an Economy of Permanence." Talk given 25 April 1981 (no location given). E. F. Schumacher Library.
10. Ibid.
11. Hannum. *People, Land, and Community.*
12. *E. F. Schumacher Society Spring Newsletter 1985.* E. F. Schumacher Library.
13. *E. F. Schumacher Society Newsletter Autumn 2002.* E. F. Schumacher Library.
14. Ward Morehouse. *Community Revitalization in North America: An Account of the First Seminar on Tools for Community Economic Transformation.* Intermediate Technology Development Group, n.d. E. F. Schumacher Library.
15. Ibid.
16. Thelma O'Brien. "Scrip Becoming Popular Alternative to Loans." *The Berkshire Record*, 26 April 1991.
17. Robert Pease. "Promoting regional enterprise: SHARE loans benefit small, local business ventures." *Christian Science Monitor*, 3 November 1986.
18. Robert Swann. "Borsodi's Search for Honest Money." *Green Revolution*, Vol. 40 No. 3, Fall 1983.
19. Susan Witt. E-mail to the author, 29 February 2009.
20. Jane Jacobs. "The Economy of Regions." Presented at the Third Annual E. F. Schumacher Lectures, South Hadley, Massachusetts, October 1983.
21. Kirkpatrick Sale. "Mother of All: An Introduction to Bioregionalism." Presented at the Third Annual E. F. Schumacher Lectures, South Hadley, Massachusetts, October 1983.
22. Jay Rossier. "The Fund for Affordable Housing: Facilitating Broad-Based Local Investment." *Catalyst*, Spring 1988.
23. Kate O'Brien. "Projects in Progress: Three Case Studies." *Journal of Light Construction*, February 1989.
24. Derek Gentile. "New affordable housing concept becomes reality in Barrington." *The Berkshire Eagle*, 27 July 1987.
25. Rossier. "The Fund for Affordable Housing."
26. K. O'Brien. "Projects in Progress."
27. Rossier. "The Fund for Affordable Housing."
28. Susan Witt. Conversation with the author, 26 February 2009.
29. Robert Swann. Interview by the author, 31 August 2001.

30. Robert Swann. "The Need for Local Currencies." Presented at the Eighth Annual E. F. Schumacher Lectures, Great Barrington, Massachusetts, October 1988, p. 3.
31. Ibid., p. 7.
32. Ibid., p. 9.
33. Ibid., pp. 12–13.
34. Ibid., p. 14.
35. Ibid., pp. 14–15.
36. Ibid., p. 16.
37. T. O'Brien. "Scrip Becoming Popular Alternative to Loans."
38. Susan Witt. "Printing Money, Making Change." *Orion Afield*, Autumn 1998.
39. Robert Swann and Susan Witt. "Dear Friends of the E. F. Schumacher Society." Membership letter, July 1992. E. F. Schumacher Library.
40. Mongillo and Booth. *Environmental Activists*, p. 302.
41. Susan Witt. Conversation with the author, 22 September 2002.
42. Thomas H. Greco. *New Money for Healthy Communities.* Thomas H. Greco Jr., 1994.
43. Susan Witt. Conversation with the author, 26 February 2009.
44. Ibid.
45. Ibid.
46. Susan Witt. Conversation with the author, 22 September 2002.
47. Juanita Nelson. "Celebration of Bob Swann's Life." Presented in Lenox, Massachusetts, 11 September 2002.
48. Susan Witt. "Stirred by Promise and Necessity."
49. Dhyana (née Barbara) Swann. Interview.
50. "From the Editors." *Orion*, March/April 2003.
51. Susan Witt. Conversation with the author, 5 August 2009.
52. *Robert Swann: Tributes.* E. F. Schumacher Society, 2003, p. 12.
53. Stephanie Mills. Notes taken during the memorial service for Robert Swann, 29 March 2003, First Congregational Church, Great Barrington, Massachusetts.

Index

Page numbers in italics refer to photographs.

About the Author

Since her galvanic Mills College commencement address in 1969, Stephanie Mills has been speaking, editing, writing, and organizing for ecology and social change. A longtime bioregionalist and veteran of the *Whole Earth* publications, Mills has written scores of essays and articles appearing in periodicals from *Glamour* to *Resurgence* and numerous anthologies. She has produced seven books, including *Epicurean Simplicity* and *Tough Little Beauties*. Mills recently helped launch a local currency in northwest Lower Michigan, where she has lived since 1984. She holds an honorary doctorate from her alma mater and is a Fellow of the Post Carbon Institute. More information about Stephanie Mills can be found at SMillsWriter.com

Gary Howe